Small Hands at War
Children in the Military

Editor

Joseph Dayton

Scribbles

Year of Publication 2018

ISBN : 9789352979691

Book Published by

Scribbles

(An Imprint of Alpha Editions)

email - alphaedis@gmail.com

Produced by: PediaPress GmbH
Limburg an der Lahn
Germany
http://pediapress.com/

Contents

Introduction

Children in the military are children (defined by the Convention on the Rights of the Child as persons under the age of 18) who are associated with military organisations, such as state armed forces and non-state armed groups. Throughout history and in many cultures, children have been involved in military campaigns. For example, thousands of children participated on all sides of the First World War and the Second World War. Children may be trained and used for combat, assigned to support roles such as porters or messengers, or used for tactical advantage as human shields or for political advantage in propaganda. Children are easy targets for military recruitment due to their greater susceptibility to influence compared to adults. Some are recruited by force while others choose to join up, often to escape poverty or because they expect military life to offer a rite of passage to maturity. Child recruits who survive armed conflict frequently suffer psychiatric illness, poor literacy and numeracy, and behavioural problems such as heightened aggression, leading to a high risk of poverty and unemployment in adulthood. Research in the UK and US has also found that the enlistment of adolescent children, even when they are not sent to war, is accompanied by a higher risk of attempted suicide, stress-related mental disorders, alcohol misuse, and violent behaviour. A number of treaties have sought to curb the participation of children in armed conflicts. According to Child Soldiers International these agreements have helped to reduce child recruitment, but the practice remains widespread and children continue to participate in hostilities around the world. Some economically powerful nations continue to rely on military recruits aged 16 or 17, and the use of younger children in armed conflict has increased in recent years as militant Islamist movements and the groups fighting them recruited children in large numbers.

History

History of children in the military

Part of a series on
Child soldiers
Main articles
• Child soldiers • History of child soldiers • Impact • Rehabilitation and reintegration
Issues
• Child abduction • Child sexual abuse • Forced marriage • Forced prostitution • Post traumatic stress disorder
Instances (examples)
• World War II • Africa • Central African Republic • Democratic Republic of Congo • India • Myanmar • Sierra Leone • Somalia • Sri Lanka
Legal aspects
• Paris Principles • Convention on the Rights of the Child • Optional protocol
Movement to end the use of child soldiers
• Red Hand Day

- v
- t
- e[1]

Part of a series on
War

- v
- t
- e[2]

Part of a series on
Slavery

- v
- t
- e[3]

Children in the military are children (defined by the Convention on the Rights of the Child as persons under the age of 18) who are associated with military organizations, such as state armed forces and non-state armed groups.

Figure 1: *A Chinese Nationalist soldier, age 10, from the Chinese Army in India waiting to board a plane in Burma, May 1944*

Throughout history and in many cultures, children have been involved in military campaigns. For example, thousands of children participated on all sides of the First World War and the Second World War.[4] Children may be trained and used for combat, assigned to support roles such as porters or messengers, or used for tactical advantage as human shields or for political advantage in propaganda.

Children are easy targets for military recruitment due to their greater susceptibility to influence compared to adults. Some children are recruited by force while others choose to join up, often to escape poverty or because they expect military life to offer a rite of passage to maturity.

Pre-20th century

Throughout history and in many cultures, children have been extensively involved in military campaigns.

The earliest mentions of minors being involved in wars come from antiquity. It was customary for youths in the Mediterranean basin to serve as aides, charioteers and armor bearers to adult warriors. Examples of this practice can be found in the Bible, such as David's service to King Saul, in Hittite and

Figure 2: *Mexico honors its cadets who died in the Battle of Chapultepec (1847).*

Figure 3: *A powder monkey on a Union vessel, American Civil War.*

ancient Egyptian art, and in ancient Greek mythology (such as the story of Hercules and Hylas), philosophy and literature.Wikipedia:Citation needed In a practice dating back to antiquity, children were routinely taken on a campaign, together with the rest of a military man's family, as part of the baggage.Wikipedia:Citation needed

The Roman Empire made use of youths in war, though it was understood that it was unwise and cruel to use children in war, and Plutarch implies that regulations required youths to be at least sixteen years of age.Wikipedia:Citation needed Despite this, several Roman legionaries were known to have enlisted aged 14 in the Imperial Roman army, such as Quintus Postunius Solus who completed 21 years of service in Legio XX Valeria Victrix, and Caecilius Donatus who served 26 years in the Legio XX and died shortly before his honorable discharge.

In medieval Europe young boys from about twelve years of age were used as military aides ("squires"), though in theory their role in actual combat was limited. The so-called Children's Crusade in 1212 recruited thousands of children as untrained soldiers under the assumption that divine power would enable them to conquer the enemy, although none of the children entered combat. According to the legend, they were instead sold into slavery. While most scholars no longer believe that the Children's Crusade consisted solely, or even mostly, of children, it nonetheless exemplifies an era in which entire families took part in a war effort.Wikipedia:Citation needed

Young boys often took part in battles during early modern warfare. When Napoleon was faced with invasion by a massive Allied force in 1814 he conscripted many teenagers for his armies. Orphans of the Imperial Guard fought in the Netherlands with Marshal MacDonald and were between the ages of 14 and 17.[5] Many of the conscripts who reported to the ranks in 1814 were referred to as Marie Louises after the Empress Marie Louise of France; they were also known as "The Infants of the Emperor". These soldiers were in their mid-teens.[6] One of their more visible roles was as the ubiquitous "drummer boy".

During the age of sail, young boys formed part of the crew of British Royal Navy ships and were responsible for many essential tasks including bringing powder and shot from the ship's magazine to the gun crews. These children were called "powder monkeys."Wikipedia:Citation needed

During the American Civil War a young boy, Bugler John Cook, served in the US Army at the age of 15 and received the Medal of Honor for his acts during the Battle of Antietam, the bloodiest day in American history.[7] Several other minors, including 11-year-old Willie Johnston, have also received the Medal of Honor.

Figure 4: *Drummer boy John Clem during the American Civil War.*

By a law signed by Nicholas I of Russia in 1827 a disproportionate number of Jewish boys, known as the cantonists, were forced into military training establishments to serve in the army. The 25-year conscription term officially commenced at the age of 18, but boys as young as eight were routinely taken to fulfill the quota. Wikipedia:Citation needed

In the final stages of the Paraguayan War, children fought in the Battle of Acosta Ñu against the Allied forces of Brazil, Argentina and Uruguay. The day is commemorated as a national holiday in Paraguay.Wikipedia:Citation needed

During the Boshin War, the pro-*shōgun* Aizu Domain formed the *Byakkotai* (白虎隊 , "White Tiger Force"), which was made up of the 16 to 17-year-old sons of Aizu samurai. During the Battle of Bonari Pass and the Battle of Aizu they fought the Satcho forces who supported the Imperial cause. A detached unit of Byakkotai was cut off from the rest of the unit and retreated to Iimori Hill, which overlooked Aizu-Wakamatsu Castle. From there, they saw what they thought was the castle on fire. 20 of the detached unit committed *seppuku* while one was unsuccessful. He was saved by a local peasant.Wikipedia:Citation needed

Figure 5: *Momčilo Gavrić and another soldier reporting to major Stevan Tucović, 1916.*

World War I

The youngest known soldier of World War I was Momčilo Gavrić, who joined the 6th Artillery Division of the Serbian Army at the age of 8, after Austro-Hungarian troops in August 1914 killed his parents, grandmother, and seven of his siblings.[8]

In the West, boys as young as 12 were caught up in the overwhelming tide of patriotism and in huge numbers enlisted for active service. Others enlisted to avoid harsh and dreary lives. Typically many were able to pass themselves off as older men, such as George Thomas Paget, who at 17 joined a Bantam battalion in the Welsh Regiment. The last surviving combat veteran of the War was Claude Choules, who enlisted in the Royal Navy at age 14 and saw his first action at the Battle of Jutland at 15.Wikipedia:Citation needed In the Gallipoli campaign, otherwise known as "Çanakkale", children as young as 15 fought in the trenches. 120 children fought in the "15'liler" or "The 15s" company, with no known survivors.Wikipedia:Citation needed

Spanish Civil War

Many child soldiers fought in the Spanish Civil War: <templatestyles src="Template:Quote/styles.css"/>

Figure 6: *Child soldiers during the Warsaw Uprising*

The centuria was an untrained mob composed mostly of boys in their teens. Here and there in the militia you came across children as young as eleven or twelve, usually refugees from Fascist territory who had been enlisted as militiamen as the easiest way of providing for them. As a rule, they were employed on light work in the rear, but sometimes they managed to worm their way to the front line, where they were a public menace. I remember one little brute throwing a hand-grenade into the dug-out fire 'for a joke'. At Monte Pocero I do not think there was anyone younger than fifteen, but the average age must have been well under twenty. Boys of this age ought never to be used in the front line, because they cannot stand the lack of sleep which is inseparable from trench warfare. At the beginning it was almost impossible to keep our position properly guarded at night. The wretched children of my section could only be roused by dragging them out of their dug-outs feet foremost, and as soon as your back was turned they left their posts and slipped into shelter; or they would even, in spite of the frightful cold, lean up against the wall of the trench and fall fast asleep.

—George Orwell

World War II

In World War II children under the age of 18 were widely used by all sides in formal and informal military roles. Children were readily indoctrinated into the prevailing ideology of the warring parties, quickly trained, and often sent to the front line; many were wounded or killed. The lack of a legal definition of a child, combined with the absence of a system for verifying the ages of prospective child recruits, contributed to the extensive use of children in the war.

After World War II: Historical examples by region

These are historical examples. For instances of children in the military today, see Children in the military.

Africa

Algeria

During the Algerian civil war (1991–2002) children were recruited frequently by Islamist armed groups fighting the government. A government-allied militia—the Legitimate Defence Groups (LDG)—also used children, according to some reports. Although the rules for joining the LDG were the same as the army, in which only adults were recruited (by conscription) the LDG applied no safeguards to ensure that children could not join up. The extent of child recruitment during the war remains unknown.

Burundi

Children were kidnapped and used extensively during the civil war of 1993–2005. In 2004 hundreds of child soldiers were in the Forces Nationales pour la Libération (FNL), an armed rebel, Hutu group.[9] Children between the ages of 10 and 16 were also conscripted by the Burundese military.

After the Arusha peace accord of 2001 and the Pretoria agreement of 2003 eventually brought the conflict to an end in 2005, the new constitution committed to not using children in direct combat. The parties to the conflict no longer recruited children in large numbers, but many remained active in the FNL, which had denounced the peace accord.

By 2006, a reintegration program organized by UNICEF had led to the release of 3,000 children from the military and armed groups. According to Child Soldiers International:

The majority of those [children] who took part in the program returned to farm and fish in their local communities, but nearly 600 returned to school. Some 1,800 former child soldiers received occupational training. Health care was provided for those with special needs and psychosocial support was provided through individual and group meetings.

As of 2017[10], Burundi no longer appears on the UN list of countries where children are used in hostilities.

Chad

Between 2007 and 2012, children were used extensively by the Chadian military as participants in armed conflict. They were also integrated into various rebel forces, including the United Front for Democratic Change (*Front Uni pour le Changement*, FUC), local self-defense forces known as *Tora Boro* militias, and two Sudanese rebel movements operating in Chad: the Justice and Equality Movement (JEM) and the G-19 faction of the Sudanese Liberation Army (SLA). After the government signed an action plan with the United Nations, children were released from service and were no longer recruited. By 2014, Chad had been removed from the UN list of countries that use child soldiers in war.

Côte d'Ivoire

During Côte d'Ivoire's civil war of 2002–2004, "children were recruited, often forcibly, by both sides",[11] and were also abducted by armed groups fighting the civil war in Liberia between 1999 and 2003. The *Patriotic Youth* – armed groups that included children in large numbers – received the active support of the government. Thousands of children saw membership of an armed group on either side of the war as a way to earn a living, although they were often unpaid, having to acquire money through extortion or begging. They were provided with automatic weapons, and girls were frequently abducted as sex slaves.

Attempts to reach a peace agreement repeatedly failed, and although after 2006 children were gradually released from military groups, approximately 2,000 children remained. After President Laurent Gbagbo refused to recognise the 2010 election result, fighting flared up again and child recruitment increased. Under the new government, however, the UN brokered an Action Plan that included the release of all children and, in 2015, the UN reported that children were no longer recruited in the country.

Eritrea

During its 30-year war for independence with Ethiopia (1961–1991) the Eritrean People's Liberation Front was "widely acknowledged" to have used children extensively as soldiers, according to the Coalition to Stop the Use of Child Soldiers (now Child Soldiers International). Once independence had been won, the Eritrean armed forces recruited and used children again during the two-year border war with Ethiopia in 1998. There were many reports of child recruitment and use (including conscription from age 15), but there is little information today about the extent of the practice, which is due in part to the absence of effective birth registration and age-verification system at the time.

The UN reported in 2002 that children were no longer being used systematically by the Eritrean armed forces, and the government acceded to the Optional Protocol on the involvement of children in armed conflict in 2005. Child recruitment continued, however; Human Rights Concern Eritrea reported in 2013 that all schoolchildren in 11th grade (approx. age 16) were made to spend the year at a military training camp, after which they were routinely recruited into the armed forces.

Ethiopia

According to the Coalition to Stop the Use of Child Soldiers in 2001 there were "credible reports" that the Ethiopian armed forces used thousands of children in its two-year border war with Eritrea between 1998 and 2000:

> *Testimonies of former child soldiers, NGOs and journalists provide evidence of child deployment on the front lines and in massive waves across mine fields... Recruitment reportedly focused on Oromos and Somalis... and on grades 9 to 12 of secondary schools.*

Children were also forcibly recruited in groups from public places. The lack of a functioning birth registration system has made it difficult to estimate the number of children affected, but it is clear that the use of children was widespread; for example, most Ethiopian prisoners of war in one large prisoner of war camp in Eritrea were estimated to be aged 14–18.

The main opposition group in the 1990s, the Oromo Liberation Front, also systematically recruited children, including by force.

In 2008 it was reported that children were no longer used for military purposes in Ethiopia, and in 2014 the government ratified the Optional Protocol on the involvement of children in armed conflict.

Figure 7: *Unidentified rebel fighters during the Second Liberian Civil War, 1999–2003.*

Liberia

In Liberia's civil wars (1989–1995, 1999–2003) all factions abducted children for direct combat, forced labour, and sexual slavery. It was the common practice of commanders to give children drugs and threaten them with execution in order to enhance their obedience; for example, soldiers were frequently given valium before a battle, known as "bubbles" or "10-10". Children were often persuaded or forced to commit grave human rights violations against civilians, including rape, torture, and the abduction of other children for military use. Children as young as 10 were used in direct combat.

United Nations disarmament, demobilisation and reintegration programs repeatedly failed when children quitted them, often to return to their former military unit, and after fighters rioted in protest at the absence of a financial reward for being disarmed. A chronic lack of resources for reintegration also prompted child soldiers to enrol in other armed groups as a means of gainful employment. By 2004 more than 20,000 children needed to be demobilised and reunited with their communities. However, by October 2004 10,000 children had been released from their military units and were part of reintegration programs.

By 2006 children were no longer being used by any military groups in the country, although armed groups from Côte d'Ivoire and Guinea continued to

Figure 8: *Displaced children in the Democratic Republic of the Congo at risk of recruitment by Rwandese armed groups and local armed bandits.*

abduct Liberian children. As of 2018[10], children were no longer being used for military purposes in Liberia, and its armed forces were recruiting only adults over the age of 18.

The use of child soldiers in Liberia was epitomised by The Small Boys Unit, established by Liberian President Charles Taylor. The boys were not provided with sustenance, but were expected to engage in "snake patrol", looting surrounding villages. Taylor and others were later tried before the Special Court for Sierra Leone because of his involvement in recruiting child soldiers.

Rwanda

An estimated 20,000 children took part in hostilities during the 1990s, including the 1994 Rwanda genocide when many children were involved in committing atrocities. 5,000 children were in the national army, while others, including many street children, joined or were made to join armed groups. After the genocide, 4,500 children were detained on suspicion of participating in atrocities, and were incarcerated for several years without charge or trial; some were sent to the Gitagata Re-Education Centre for males below 14 years of age. In the late 1990s, children were widely recruited again, often by force, to fight in the Democratic Republic of the Congo (DRC).[12]

Initial demobilisation and reintegration programmes failed after many schools banned former child soldiers and a high rate of unemployment rendered them vulnerable to re-recruitment by militia groups. In 2003, as the Rwandan military presence in the DRC reduced, so did the demand for child soldiers. The government introduced new legislation to raise the minimum enlistment age 18 and the armed forces stopped recruiting children. Nonetheless, armed groups continued to do so, albeit to a reduced extent, for their operations in the DRC.

Sierra Leone

During the Sierra Leone Civil War (1991–2002) thousands of children were recruited by government armed forces and non-government armed groups, particularly the anti-government Revolutionary United Front (RUF) and the Armed Forces Revolutionary Council (AFRC), and the pro-government Civil Defence Forces (CDF).

Children were often forcibly recruited, given drugs and used to commit atrocities. Thousands of girls were also recruited as soldiers and often subjected to sexual exploitation. Many of the children were survivors of attacks on villages, which were routinely ordered to hand over their children to armed groups. By 2001, an estimated 10,000 children were being used for military purposes by government armed forces and various armed groups, particularly the RUF.

After 2002, when the war was declared over, an extensive United Nations disarmament, demobilisation and reintegration programme reunited most former child soldiers with their communities, although it drew criticism for neglecting the needs of women and girls.

In June 2007 the Special Court for Sierra Leone found three men from the rebel Armed Forces Revolutionary Council (AFRC) guilty of war crimes, crimes against humanity, and other serious violations of international humanitarian law, including the recruitment of children under the age of 15 years into the armed forces. With this the Special Court became the first ever UN-backed tribunal to secure a conviction for the military conscription of children.[13]

As of 2018[10], children were no longer being used for military purposes in Sierra Leone, and its armed forces were recruiting only adults over the age of 18.

In his book *A Long Way Gone: Memoirs of a Child Soldier*, Ishmael Beah chronicles his life during the conflict in Sierra Leone. In *Armies of the Young: Child Soldiers in War and Terrorism* anthropologist David M. Rosen discusses the murders, rapes, tortures, and thousands of amputations committed by the RUF Small Boys Unit. The film *Blood Diamond* is set during the civil war. The issue is also explored in the *Bones* episode, *The Survivor In The Soap*.

Figure 9: *David Livingstone speaks about his experiences as a child soldier with the Lord's Resistance Army in Uganda.*

Uganda

Over a period of twenty years the rebel Lord's Resistance Army (LRA) has abducted more than 30,000 boys and girls as soldiers or sex slaves. Joseph Kony began the Lord's Resistance Army (LRA) in 1987, originally to protect northern Ugandans from the 1986 military coup by the People's National Resistance Army,. Stating that he "received messages from God" Kony began attacking his own people, the Acholi, to establish a new theocratic government in Uganda based on the principles of the "Ten Commandments of God". This attempt by the LRA to gain control of the Ugandan government via roaming armies used boy- as well as girl-children as soldiers, such as Grace Akallo.

The LRA expansion into South Sudan, the Central African Republic and the Democratic Republic of Congo has used large numbers of children as active combatants and participants in extreme violence. On the 21 October 2008 an appeal by the UN Security Council was made asking for the LRA to cease all military action in the DRC immediately. On 14 June 2002 Uganda deposited its instrument of ratification of the Rome Statute, and on 16 December 2003 the Government of Uganda referred the situation concerning northern Uganda to the prosecutor of the International Criminal Court (ICC). The ICC investigated the situation and on 14 October 2005 issued indictments against Lord's Resistance Army leader Joseph Kony and four other commanders for war crimes: Vincent Otti; Raska Lukwiya (indictment terminated, deceased);

Figure 10: *Rebel Salvadoran soldier boy combatant in Perquin, El Salvador 1990, during the Salvadoran Civil War.*

Okot Odhiambo; and Dominic Ongwen. The warrant for Kony, Otti and Odhiambo includes the alleged crime of the forced enlisting of children contrary to the Rome Statute Art. 8(2) (e)(vii).[14]

The National Resistance Army also made use of child soldiers. Between 2003 and 2007, non-state armed groups fighting the LRA also used children.

In 2007 the Ugandan government agreed an action plan with the UN to end the use of child soldiers and in 2008 the country no longer appeared on the UN list of countries that recruit and use children.

Americas

El Salvador

During the civil war between 1980 and 1992 the Salvadoran military and the main opposition group, the *Frente Farabundo Martí de Liberación National* (FMLN), recruited children extensively. The recruitment was frequently carried out by force and focused on economically suppressed regions. A fifth of the army's personnel were aged under 18, as were a quarter of the FMLN. In a group of 278 former FMLN child soldiers interviewed for a study, the average age of recruitment was 10 years. The large majority of child recruits

Figure 11: *Detail of a propaganda mural chowing a child soldier from the Iran-Iraq War, in Ardabil, Iranian Azerbaijan.*

on both sides were living in poverty, and had been largely deprived of formal education. Many children who were not recruited by force joined of their own volition, mainly either to improve their circumstances or because they believed in the cause.

After the civil war came to a close, rehabilitation and reintegration programmes for children mostly failed; the majority of FMLN children were not involved in them, and the large majority of those who were dropped out of them. A decade after the peace accord former child soldiers were still experiencing nightmares, depression, anxiety, and related signs of psychiatric trauma.

Today, the Salvadoran military no longer sends children to war, but it still recruits and trains them from the age of 16.

Middle East

Iran

During the Iran–Iraq War (1980–1988) the armed forces used children widely; the extent of the practice is not known but the number of children involved is thought to be in the tens of thousands. Armed groups associated with the government advertised widely for children from age 14 to join them, and the country's Supreme Leader, Ayatollah Khomeini, urged children to fight at the front. According to the Coalition to Stop the Use of Child Soldiers (now Child Soldiers International):

> *Ayatollah Khomeini declared that parental permission was unnecessary for those going to the front, that volunteering for military duty was a religious obligation, and that serving in the armed forces took priority over all other forms of work or study. Various sources reported that children were indoctrinated into participating in combat. They were given "keys to paradise" and promised that they would go directly to heaven if they died as martyrs against the Iraqi enemy.*

The children involved were overwhelmingly from slums and poor villages, and some participated without the knowledge of their parents, including Mohammad Hossein Fahmideh. Thousands of children took part in human wave attacks, leading to widespread deaths and injuries. The total number of all Iranian casualties is estimated to be 200,000–600,000,[15,16,17,18,19,20] of which approximately a third were aged 15–19 (and 3 percent under 14), according to one assessment.

After the war, the *Basij,* an official militia organisation, continued to recruit children from age 15, focusing on those living in poverty and sometimes recruiting them by force. In 2004, the *Basij* was estimated to have as many as a million members of all ages. *Ansar-e Hizbollah*, an armed group tolerated by the government, also recruited children widely in the 2000s, with no age restriction. As of 2018[10], the Iranian armed forces continue to enlist from age 16 and the government has not yet ratified the Optional Protocol on the involvement of children in armed conflict.

Iraq

The government of Saddam Hussein maintained 'boot camps' of civilian youths between the ages of 12 and 17 that involved small arms training and Ba'athist political indoctrination. Iraqi opposition sources and the US State Department reported that children who refused faced punishment. The state incorporated children as young as ten into the *Futuwah* and *Ashbal Saddam* youth movements and then subjected them to military training, sometimes for 14 hours a day. P. W. Singer has compared the groups to the *Hitler Jugend*. In the Gulf War 12-year-old boys fought for the Iraqis. Children also participated in the Iran–Iraq War.

In the 2003 invasion of Iraq, US forces fought children at Nasariya, Karbala, and Kirkuk, and the US sent captured child combatants to Abu Ghraib prison. In 2009 a UN report on the post-war Iraqi occupation stated that the Iraqi insurgency had used children as combatants; it noted, for example, a suicide attack against Kirkuk's police commander by a boy aged between 10 and 13.

Figure 12: *Child dressed as Khmer Rouge soldier.*

Asia

Cambodia

In the 1970s the *Khmer Rouge* exploited thousands of desensitised, conscripted children in their early teens to commit mass murder and other atrocities during the Cambodian civil war and subsequent genocide. The indoctrinated children were taught to follow any order without hesitation. After it was deposed in 1979, the *Khmer Rouge* fought a guerrilla war against the new government, and until at least 1998 relied heavily on child recruits, including forced recruitment by abduction. During this period, the children were deployed mainly in unpaid support roles, such as ammunition-carriers, and also as combatants.

Cambodia's state armed forces also recruited children widely. Throughout the 1990s the army was recruiting children from the age of 10 and using them in armed conflict, mainly as porters and spies, and also as combatants. Four percent of the army were children, according to an estimate in the *Cambodia Daily*. Many children had fled the *Khmer Rouge* without a means to feed themselves and hoped that joining the government forces would enable them to survive, although local commanders frequently denied them any pay. Children often capitalised on the lack of an effective birth registration system to lie about their age in order to enlist. Other children, some as young as 8, were forced to join.

Figure 13: *Former child soldiers at a centre for rehabilitation and reintegration into their communities, Sri Lanka.*

By 2000, the Cambodian government had signed the Optional Protocol on
the Involvement of Children in Armed Conflict and its armed forces resolved
to recruit adults only. Meanwhile, the *Khmer Rouge* had collapsed with the
death of its leader, Pol Pot, in 1998. By 2004, children were no longer being
recruited in the country, although the demobilisation programmes were inade-
quate, according to UNICEF, failing to offer appropriate rehabilitative support
to released children.

Sri Lanka

Between 1983 and 2009 Sri Lanka's government fought a civil war with the
Liberation Tigers of Tamil Eelam (Tamil Tigers). For its entire duration the
Tamil Tigers and other armed groups made routine use of child recruits, typically aged 14–17 and sometimes under 10.[21] Some children enlisted to escape
deprivation or racism, or during compulsory military training at their school
when they were exposed to recruitment propaganda. Others were recruited
by force when walking home from school or after the Tigers pressurised families to surrender one child, as per its policy. In 2001, international sources
estimated that 40 percent of Tamil Tiger personnel were children, contrary to
official statements insisting that the organisation did not use them. Sri Lankan

soldiers nicknamed one unit the "Baby Battalion", due to the number of children in it. Although state armed forces recruited only adults over the age of 18, they supported the Karuna group, a Tamil splinter organisation opposed to the Tamil Tigers, to recruit children by force. The government also used detained Tamil Tiger children for propaganda by exposing them to the media.

The first international initiative to demobilise and reintegrate children into their communities began in 2003, but was halted in 2004 because the Tigers failed to keep their commitment to release children from their ranks. The organisation began to release children in 2004, but continued to enlist several thousand, albeit in progressively smaller numbers, until at least 2007. The Tamil Tigers were defeated in 2009 and all other parties to the conflict stopped recruiting children in the same year.

Europe

Chechnya/Russia

During the First Chechen War, Chechen separatist forces included a large number of boys and girls, some as young as 11. According to the UN: "Child soldiers in Chechnya were reportedly assigned the same tasks as adult combatants, and served on the front lines soon after joining the armed forces." In 2004 under-18s were still believed to be involved in a range of armed groups in the war against Russia; some allegedly took part in suicide bombings.[22]

United Kingdom

Children aged 17 were sent to the Falklands War in 1982 (where three were killed) and the Gulf War in 1990–91 (where two were killed). 17-year-olds were also deployed as NATO peacekeepers in the former Yugoslavia during the 1990s. Having initially resisted international negotiations to prevent the deployment of children, the UK agreed to deploy adults only when it signed the Optional Protocol on the Involvement of Children in Armed Conflict in 2000, but remained committed to recruiting and training children from age 16. Between 2003 and 2010 22 personnel aged 17 were sent to Afghanistan and Iraq, reportedly in error.

During the Troubles in Northern Ireland (c. 1960s to 1998) it was common for paramilitary groups to recruit and use children, including as combatants. Five children in Republican paramilitary groups, seven in Loyalist paramilitary groups, and five in the British armed forces, died during the conflict. The youngest, Cathleen McCartland, was recruited by the Irish Republican Army (IRA) and was aged 12 when she was killed in Belfast.

External links

Reference: Child soldiers worldwide

- Child Soldiers World Index[23] (2018), child soldier world map and statistics
- Child Soldiers International, historical reports:
  - Child Soldiers Global Report: 2001[24]
  - Child Soldiers Global Report: 2004[25]
  - Child Soldiers Global Report: 2008[26]
  - Louder than words: 2012[27]

Impact

Impact of war on children

- $\underline{v}$
- $\underline{t}$
- $\underline{e}^{28}$

The number of children in armed conflict zones are around 250 million. They confront physical and mental harms from war experiences.

"Armed conflict" is defined in two ways according to International Humanitarian Law: "1) international armed conflicts, opposing two or more States, 2) non-international armed conflicts, between governmental forces and nongovernmental armed groups, or between such groups only."

Children in war-zones may act as perpetrators, becoming child soldiers. It is estimated that there are around 300,000 child soldiers around the world and 40 percent of them are girls. Children are also victims of armed conflicts. They are forced to evacuate, serve as child soldier, suffer from sexually transmitted diseases and are deprived of education opportunities.

Background

See also: Childhood in war

The presence of children in the war can go back to Middle Ages and Napoleonic Wars. Children fought in the American Civil war, significantly contributed to the Battle of New Market which was fought in Virginia (May 15, 1864). Children were also fighting in the World War II, especially noted to serve as "Hitler Youth". However, in modern days, the number of child victims is increasing as the proportion of civilian casualties is also increasing. In 18th, 19th, and early 20th centuries, about half the war victims were civilians while it was almost 90 percent by the end of the 1980s. Children compose a large part of the population affected by wars, data from the American Psychology Association show of the 95 percent of civilians killed in recent years' by modern armed conflicts, approximately 50 percent of them were children.

According to United Nations Children's Fund (UNICEF), the estimated casualties of children during the last decade was: "2 million killed, 4-5 million disabled, 12 million left homeless, more than 1 million orphaned or separated from their parents, and some 10 million psychologically traumatized". Currently, there are over two million child refugees fleeing from Syria and over 870,000 refugees from Somalia. Among 100,000 people who have been killed in Syria, at least 10,000 were children.

Potential risk factors of war on children

Direct exposure to violence

Death and injury

By being directly exposed to violence such as bombing and combats, children are killed during conflicts. In 2017 alone, there were 1,210 terrorist attacks around the world, mostly happening in Middle East region and 8,074 fatalities. There were nine terrorist incidents with more than hundred deaths in conflict zones. Under the Trump administration, civilian casualties from the United States armed forces are at all-time high in Syria and Iraq. Also, children are more likely to be injured by landmines. Twenty percent of landmine victims are children in mine-affected countries. They are often intrigued by colorful appeaanace of landmines and explosives. Children can lose sights or hearing; lose body parts; suffer from the trauma. At least 8,605 people were killed or injured by landmines in 2016 and 6,967 casulities in 2015. Most of them were civilians and 42 percent of civilian casualties were children and the number of child casualties were at least 1,544 in 2016.

Sexual violence

The United Nations define the term "conflict-related sexual violence" as "rape, sexual slavery, forced prostitution, forced pregnancy, forced abortion, enforced sterilization, forced marriage, and any other form of sexual violence of comparable gravity perpetrated against women, men, girls or boys that is directly or indirectly linked to a conflict". More than 20,000 Muslim girls and women have been raped in Bosnia since 1992. Many cases in Rwanda show that every surviving adolescent girl was raped. Sexual violence also causes sexually transmitted diseases – such as HIV/AIDS – to spread. One of the factors is involvement with military forces as they sexually abuse and exploit girls and women during conflicts. Besides, as HIV-positive mothers give birth to HIV-infected children without anti-retroviral drugs, the prevalence of HIV/AIDS tend to spread fast.

Unmet basic needs during warfare

War disrupts the supply of necessities to children and their families like food, water, shelter, health services, and education. Lack of access to these basic needs may deprive children of their physical, social-emotional, and psychological development. In case of South Sudan, constant violent conflicts along with climate shocks greatly damaged the agriculture-based economy. As a result, more than 1.1 million children are suffering from severe food shortages. In countries across Africa and the Middle East, over 2.5 million children are suffering from severe acute malnutrition. Economic sanctions such as trade restrictions from international community and organizations may play a role in serious economic hardship and deterioration of infrastructure in armed conflict zones. This makes it extremely difficult for children to survive as they are usually in the most bottom level of socioeconomic status. As of 2001, around half a million Iraqi children were predicted to be dead due to sanctions regime.

Detrimental parenting behavior can also affect child development. In a war context, families and communities are not able to provide an environment conducive to the children's development. Mike Wessells, Ph. D., a Randolph-Macon College psychology professor with extensive experience in war zones explained; "When parents are emotionally affected by war, that alters their ability to care for their children properly. War stresses increase family violence, creating a pattern that then gets passed on when the children become parents." Scarcity of resources increases cognitive load which affects attention span, cognitive capacity, and executive control that are critical abilities to reason and solve problems. Reduced mental and emotional capabilities caused by stress from a war can degrade their parenting capabilities and negatively change behaviors towards children.

Disruption of education also occurs with the destruction of schools during wars. The human and financial resources are compromised during crisis. The United Nations reported that more than 13 million children are deprived of education opportunities and more than 8,850 schools were destroyed because of armed conflicts in the Middle East. According to UNICEF report, In Yemen, 1.8 million children were out of education in 2015. Between 2014-2015, almost half a million children in Gaza Strip were not able to go to school because of the damages on schools. In Sudan, more than three million children cannot go to school because of the conflicts. In Mozambique, around 45 percent of primary schools were destroyed during the conflict. Fear and disruption make it hard for children and teacher to focus on education. This generates an educational gap, depriving children of essential education, building social-emotional skills, and thus reintegrating into society. In addition, gender equality can also be compromised as education disruption in armed conflict zones generally excludes girls.

Impact on psychological development of children

Brain development

Early childhood experience accounts for a large part of human brain development. Neural connections for sensory ability, language, and cognitive function are all actively made during the first year for a child. The plasticity and malleability which refer to the flexibility of the brain is highest in the early brain development years. Therefore, the brain can be readily changed by surrounding environments of children. In that sense, children in armed conflict zones may be more susceptible to mental problems such as anxiety and depression, as well as physiological problems in the immune system and central nervous systems.

Stress in early childhood can impede brain development of children that results in both physical and mental health problems.[29] Healthy brain and physical development can be hampered by excessive or prolonged activation of stress response systems. Although both adrenaline and cortisol help prepare the body for coping with stressors, when they are used to prolonged and uncontrollable stress, this stress response system can lead to impairments in both mental and physical health.

Lack of basic resources may also impede child brain development. Childhood socioeconomic status influences neural development and affects cognitive ability and mental health through adult life. Especially, poverty is regarded to deteriorate cognitive capacity. Many studies have shown that poverty in early childhood can be harmful in that poor families lack time and financial resources to invest in promoting child development. This suggests that the serious deprivation of resources in armed conflict zones is extremely detrimental to cognitive development of children during warfare.

Okasha and Elkholy (2012) have theorized that psychological immunization can help children who are frequently exposed to conflict to better acclimate themselves to the stressors of war.

Attachment theory

Children who are detached from a family in early age may go through problems regarding attachment. Children under five are more likely to experience a greater risk of depression and anxiety compared to adolescents. Attachment theory suggests that the ability of a child to create attachment can be deterred by deviant environmental conditions and reflected experiences with caregivers. Different types of attachments can be formed with different caregivers and upbringing environment. In addition, different experiences of attachment in childhood are known to be related to mental health issues in adulthood.

Other psychological impacts

Children in war-zones witness and experience horrendous violent activities which may lead to development of psychological disorders such as posttraumatic stress disorder (PTSD). By 2017, 3 million children from Syria have witnessed effects of war directly. 80% of the 94 Iraqi children exposed to the Feb 13, 1991 bombing showed PTSD symptoms. Also, study shows that 41 percent of Palestinian children from Gaza Strip suffered from PTSD. The incidence of the effects of war has a 10 to 90 percent variation in terms of developing PTSD, depression and behavioral problems. PTSD is known to have intergenerational effects.

Rehabilitation issues

Reintegration into society for child soldiers

There are around 300,000 child soldiers around the world.

Disarmament, demobilization, and reintegration (DDR) programs are conducted to rehabilitate child soldiers and war-affected children. The creation of DDR in Sierra Leone was led by UNICEF in 1999. However, disarmament consistently failed to attract female combatants who were forced to provide sexual services as they were too afraid to step forward for demobilization process.

Child soldiers are often stigmatized and confronted with discrimination from community. Reintegration and rehabilitation depends on the level of violence occurred in the region, acceptance from family and community, and resources like education and training programs to recover war-affected youth. The Paris Principles suggest extensive and detailed guildelines on reintegration of children associated with armed forces or armed groups.

Psychological treatment process

Psychological treatment is considered to be more challenging after the age of five. This is because the plasticity of the brain reduces after the age of five since much of the brain's development occurs before the age of six. Long-term psychological treatment is many times required. Some children develop resilience and are able to overcome significant adversity. Helpful community surroundings and stable caregivers are regarded as being able to build capacity to recover from adverse childhood experiences.

Intervention programs for children in war-zones

Narrative Exposure Therapy

Narrative Exposure Therapy is a short-term individual intervention for treatment of PTSD based on the cognitive-behavioral exposure therapy. KidNET is a narrative exposure therapy used with war-affected children aged 12-17 years. Under this, the mental health professional encourages the patients to describe the events of their life – from birth till present. Improvements through Kid-NET are seen in the refugee children in eastern Europe, children affected by the Rwandan genocide, and the children in Sri Lanka. **Testimonial psychotherapy** is another short-term individual treatment for the war-affected individuals in which they record their experiences with trauma. These recordings are then later analyzed by doctors along with the patients to understand how the personal experiences are connected to trauma.

Dyad Psychosocial Support

Dyad psychosocial support is a family-level treatment for mother and children affected by war aiming at the emotional and psychological development of children. One example of the program was carried out in Bosnia for a duration of 5-month in which weekly meetings of the mothers were carried out to discuss their children's development, coping mechanisms, and trauma. This program indicated net positive results in terms of the "maternal mental health, children's weight gain, and children's psychosocial functioning and mental health".

Youth Readiness Intervention Program

Youth Readiness intervention program (Sierra Leone) is aimed at youth in the war to treat emotional and psychological issues and inculcate pro-social behavior in them. A study by Betancourt et al evaluates results from Sierra Leone. It reports positive results.

Convention on the Rights of the Child

Convention on the Rights of the Child

Parties to the convention
Signed, but not ratified
Non-signatory

Signed	20 November 1989
Location	New York City
Effective	2 September 1990
Condition	20 ratifications[30]
Signatories	140
Parties	196 (all eligible states except the United States)
Depositary	UN Secretary-General[31]
Languages	Arabic, Chinese, English, French, Russian, Spanish

UN Convention on the Rights of the Child at Wikisource

Part of the Politics series on

Youth rights

- Youth rights
- Social movements portal

- v
- t
- e[32]

The United Nations **Convention on the Rights of the Child** (commonly abbreviated as the **CRC** or **UNCRC**) is a human rights treaty which sets out the civil, political, economic, social, health and cultural rights of children. The Convention defines a child as any human being under the age of eighteen, unless the age of majority is attained earlier under national legislation.

Nations that ratify this convention are bound to it by international law. Compliance is monitored by the UN Committee on the Rights of the Child, which is composed of members from countries around the world. Once a year, the Committee submits a report to the Third Committee of the United Nations General Assembly, which also hears a statement from the CRC Chair, and the Assembly adopts a Resolution on the Rights of the Child.

Governments of countries that have ratified the Convention are required to report to, and appear before, the United Nations Committee on the Rights of the Child periodically to be examined on their progress with regards to the advancement of the implementation of the Convention and the status of child rights in their country. Their reports and the committee's written views and concerns are available on the committee's website.

The UN General Assembly adopted the Convention and opened it for signature on 20 November 1989 (the 30th anniversary of its Declaration of the Rights of the Child). It came into force on 2 September 1990, after it was ratified by the required number of nations. Currently, 196 countries are party to it,[33] including every member of the United Nations except the United States.[34,35]

Two optional protocols were adopted on 25 May 2000. The First Optional Protocol restricts the involvement of children in military conflicts, and the Second Optional Protocol prohibits the sale of children, child prostitution and child pornography. Both protocols have been ratified by more than 160 states.

A third optional protocol relating to communication of complaints was adopted in December 2011 and opened for signature on 28 February 2012. It came into effect on 14 April 2014.

Contents

The Convention deals with the child-specific needs and rights. It requires that the "nations that ratify this convention are bound to it by international law". Ratifying states must act in the best interests of the child. In all jurisdictions implementing the Convention requires compliance with child custody and guardianship laws as that every child has basic rights, including the right to life, to their own name and identity, to be raised by their parents within a family or cultural grouping, and to have a relationship with both parents, even if they are separated.

The Convention obliges states to allow parents to exercise their parental responsibilities. The Convention also acknowledges that children have the right to express their opinions and to have those opinions heard and acted upon when appropriate, to be protected from abuse or exploitation, and to have their privacy protected, and it requires that their lives not be subject to excessive interference.

The Convention also obliges signatory states to provide separate legal representation for a child in any judicial dispute concerning their care and asks that the child's viewpoint be heard in such cases.

The Convention forbids capital punishment for children. In its General Comment 8 (2006) the Committee on the Rights of the Child stated that there was an "obligation of all state parties to move quickly to prohibit and eliminate all corporal punishment and all other cruel or degrading forms of punishment of children".[36] Article 19 of the Convention states that state parties must "take all appropriate legislative, administrative, social and educational measures to protect the child from all forms of physical or mental violence",[37] but it makes no reference to corporal punishment. The Committee's interpretation of this section to encompass a prohibition on corporal punishment has been rejected by several state parties to the Convention, including Australia, Canada and the United Kingdom.

The European Court of Human Rights has referred to the Convention when interpreting the European Convention on Human Rights.[38]

Global standards and cultural relativism

Global human rights standards were challenged at the World Conference on Human Rights in Vienna (1993) when a number of governments (prominently China, Indonesia, Malaysia and Iran) raised serious objections to the idea of universal human rights. There are unresolved tensions between "universalistic" and "relativistic" approaches in the establishment of standards and strategies designed to prevent or overcome the abuse of children's capacity to work.

Child marriage and slavery

Some scholars link slavery and slavery-like practices for many child marriages. Child marriage as slavery is not directly addressed by the Convention on the Rights of the Child.

States party and signatories

Currently 196 countries are parties to the treaty (some with stated reservations or interpretations). This includes every member of the United Nations (except the United States), plus the Cook Islands, Niue, the State of Palestine, and the Holy See. The United States has not ratified it. South Sudan did not sign the convention, however ratification was complete in January 2015. Somalia's domestic ratification finished in January 2015 and the instrument was deposited with the United Nations in October 2015.

All successor states of Czechoslovakia and Yugoslavia (Bosnia and Herzegovina, Croatia, Czech Republic, Macedonia, Montenegro, Serbia, Slovenia, and Slovakia) made declarations of succession to the treaty and currently apply it.

The convention does not apply in the territories of Akrotiri and Dhekelia, Gibraltar, Guernsey and Tokelau.

Azerbaijan

Azerbaijan ratified Convention on the Rights of the Child on 21 July 1992. In terms of the ratification of the Convention on the Rights of the Child, a significant number of laws, decrees and resolutions were approved in Azerbaijan by the President and the Cabinet of Ministers focusing on the development of the child welfare system. In this regard, the Convention №182 on "Elimination of the worst forms of child labour" and Recommendation №190 of the International Labour Organization and the Hague Convention on International adoption of children were ratified by Milli Majlis in 2004.

There is a concern over the administration of juvenile justice in Azerbaijan, mostly regarding compliance with articles 37, 39 and 40 of the Convention on the Rights of the Child, as well as other relevant standards such as the Beijing Rules, the Riyadh Guidelines and the United Nations Rules for the Protection of Juveniles Deprived of their Liberty. Therefore, international organizations assisted Azerbaijan to improve the situation in the field of juvenile justice. Juvenile offenders have been added to the Presidential pardons on a regular basis.

Azerbaijan has built cooperation with many international organizations, in particular with UNICEF in the field of child protection. In 1993, UNICEF began its activity in Azerbaijan. In 2005, Azerbaijan and UNICEF signed a 5-year country program. The country program for 2005-2009 was implemented in the field of child protection, children's health and nutrition, children's education and youth health, their development and participation. In addition, UNICEF supports Azerbaijan in developing juvenile justice system, establishing alternative care system and raising awareness among youth about HIV/AIDS.

Canada

Canada became a signatory to the Convention on 28 May 1990 and ratified in 1991. Youth criminal laws in Canada underwent major changes resulting in the Youth Criminal Justice Act (YCJA) which went into effect on 1 April 2003. The Act specifically refers to Canada's different commitments under the Convention. The convention was influential in the administrative Law decision of *Baker v Canada (Minister of Citizenship and Immigration)*.

India

India ratified UNCRC on 11 December 1992, agreeing in principles all articles except with certain reservations on issues relating to child labor. In India there is law that children under the age of 18 should not work, but there is no outright ban on child labor, and the practice is generally permitted in most industries except those deemed "hazardous". Although a law in October 2006 banned child labor in hotels, restaurants, and as domestic servants, there continues to be high demand for children as hired help in the home. Current estimates as to the number of child laborers in the country range from the government's conservative estimate of 4 million children under 14 years of age to the much higher estimates of children's rights activists, which hover around 60 million.Wikipedia:Citation needed Little is being done to address the problem since the economy is booming and the nuclear family is spreading, thereby increasing demand for child laborers. In India many people are still suffering from non-nutritious food, many parents are still leaving their children on riverside, in trains etc. Under the auspices of the Unicef financed Odisha initiative the Government of India is specifying the outline of a means of change and improvement in child care, and many trusts such as childLine, Plan India and savethechildren too are taking efforts to outdate child labor from India. A few of the organisations who work with children's rights in India are Plan India, CRY (Child Rights and You), Save the Children, Bal Vikas Dhara-New Delhi, Bachpan Bachao Andolan, CHORD-Hyderabad apart from them todo an organization India strives hard to protect the children .

Iran

Iran has adhered to the convention (except for alleged child slavery) since 1991 and ratified it in the Parliament in 1994. Upon ratification, Iran made the following reservation: "If the text of the Convention is or becomes incompatible with the domestic laws and Islamic standards at any time or in any case, the Government of the Islamic Republic shall not abide by it." Iran has also signed the both optional protocols which relate to the special protection of children against involvement in armed conflict and the sale of children and sexual exploitation.

Although Iran is a state party to the Convention, international human rights organisations and foreign governments[39] routinely denounced executions of Iranian child offenders as a violation of the treaty. But on 10 February 2012, Iran's parliament changed the controversial law of executing juveniles. In the new law, the age of 18 (solar year) would be for both genders considered the cut-off for adulthood and offenders under this age will be sentenced under a separate law. Based on the previous Islamic law, which was revised, girls at the age of 9 and boys at 15 (lunar year, 11 days shorter than a solar year) were fully responsible for their crimes.

"According to Islamic sources, the criterion for criminal responsibility is reaching the age of maturity which, according to the Shi'ite School of the IRI, is 9 lunar years (8 years and 9 months) for girls and 15 lunar years (14 years and 7 months) for boys."

Ireland

Ireland signed the Convention on the Rights of the Child on 30 September 1990 and ratified it, without reservation, on 28 September 1992.[40] In response to criticisms expressed in the 1998 review by the UN Committee on the Rights of the Child in Geneva, the Irish government established the office of Ombudsman for Children and drew up a national children's strategy. In 2006, following concerns expressed by the committee that the wording of the Irish Constitution does not allow the State to intervene in cases of abuse other than in very exceptional cases, the Irish government undertook to amend the constitution to make a more explicit commitment to children's rights.[41]

Israel

Israel ratified the Convention in 1991. In 2010, UNICEF criticized Israel for its failure to create a government-appointed commission on children's rights or to adopt a national children's rights strategy or program in order to implement various Israeli laws addressing children's rights. The report criticizes Israel for holding that the Convention does not apply in the West Bank and for defining as Palestinians under the age of 16 in the occupied territories as children, even though Israeli law defines a child as being under 18, in line with the Convention. A contemporaneous report by the Organization for Economic Cooperation and Development found that Israel's investment in children is below the international average and the actual investment had fallen between 1995 and 2006.[42] In 2012, the United Nations Committee on the Rights of the Child criticized Israel for its bombing attacks on Palestinians in the Gaza Strip, stating, "Destruction of homes and damage to schools, streets and other public facilities gravely affect children" and called them "gross violations of the Convention on the Rights of the Child, its Optional Protocol on the involvement of children in armed conflict and international humanitarian law". It also criticized Palestinian rocket attacks from Gaza on southern Israel which traumatized Israeli children, calling on all parties to protect children.[43]

New Zealand

New Zealand ratified the Convention on 6 April 1993 with reservations concerning the right to distinguish between persons according to the nature of their authority to be in New Zealand, the need for legislative action on economic exploitation—which it argued was adequately protected by existing law, and the provisions for the separation of juvenile offenders from adult offenders.[44]

In 1994, the Court of Appeal of New Zealand dismissed the suggestion that the Minister for Immigration and his department were at liberty to ignore the convention, arguing that this would imply that the country's adherence was "at least partly window-dressing".[45]

The Children's Commissioner Act 2003 enhanced the office of Children's Commissioner, giving it significantly stronger investigative powers. The Office of the Children's Commissioner is responsible for convening the UN-CROC Monitoring Group, which monitors the New Zealand Government's implementation of the Children's Convention, it's Optional Protocols and the Government's response to recommendations from the United Nations Committee on the Rights of the Child. The monitoring group comprises members from the Human Rights Commission (New Zealand), UNICEF New Zealand, Action for Children and Youth Aotearoa and Save the Children New Zealand.

In May 2007, New Zealand passed the Crimes (Substituted Section 59) Amendment Act 2007, which removed the defence of "reasonable force" for the purpose of correction. In its third and final vote, Parliament voted 113 to eight in favour of the legislation.

Saudi Arabia

Saudi Arabia ratified the Convention in 1996, with a reservation "with respect to all such articles as are in conflict with the provisions of Islamic law" which is the national law. The Committee on the Rights of the Child, which reviewed Saudi Arabia's treatment of children under the Convention in January 2005, strongly condemned the government for its practice of imposing the death penalty on juveniles, calling it "a serious violation of the fundamental rights". The committee said it was "deeply alarmed" over the discretionary power judges hold to treat juveniles as adults: In its 2004 report the Saudi Arabian government had stated that it "never imposes capital punishment on persons ... below the age of 18". The government delegation later acknowl-edged that a judge could impose the death penalty whenever he decided that the convicted person had reached his or her majority, regardless of the person's actual age at the time of the crime or at the time of the scheduled execution.[46]

United Kingdom

The United Kingdom ratified the Convention on 16 December 1991, with sev-eral declarations and reservations,[47] and made its first report to the Committee on the Rights of the Child in January 1995. Concerns raised by the Commit-tee included the growth in child poverty and inequality, the extent of violence towards children, the use of custody for young offenders, the low age of crim-inal responsibility, and the lack of opportunities for children and young peo-ple to express views.[48] The 2002 report of the Committee expressed similar concerns, including the welfare of children in custody, unequal treatment of asylum seekers, and the negative impact of poverty on children's rights. In September 2008, the UK government decided to withdraw its reservations and agree to the Convention in these respects.[49]

The 2002 report's criticism of the legal defence of "reasonable chastisement" of children by parents, which the Committee described as "a serious violation of the dignity of the child",[50] was rejected by the UK Government. The Minister for Children, Young People and Families commented that while fewer parents are using smacking as a form of discipline, the majority said they would not support a ban.[51]

In evidence to the Parliamentary Joint Committee on Human Rights, the Com-mittee was criticised by the Family Education Trust for "adopting radical in-terpretations of the UN Convention on the Rights of the Child in its pursuit of an agenda".[52] The Joint Committee's report recommended that "the time has come for the Government to act upon the recommendations of the UN Committee on the Rights of the Child concerning the corporal punishment of children and the incompatibility of the defence of reasonable chastisement with its obligations under the Convention."[53] The UK Government responded that "the use of physical punishment is a matter for individual parents to decide".[54]

Although child slavery is difficult to gauge within the UK, child slaves are im-ported into the UK and sold.

United States

The United States government played an active role in the drafting of the Con-vention and signed it on 16 February 1995, but has not ratified it. It has been claimed that American opposition to the Convention stems primarily from po-litical and religious conservatives.[55] For example, The Heritage Foundation sees "a civil society in which moral authority is exercised by religious congregations, family, and other private associations is fundamental to the American order".[56] and the Home School Legal Defense Association (HSLDA) argues that the CRC threatens homeschooling.

The United States had permitted the execution and life imprisonment of juvenile offenders, in contravention of the Article 37 of the Convention. In 2005, a Supreme Court decision declared juvenile executions to be unconstitutional as "cruel and unusual punishment";[57] in 2012, the Court held that mandatory sentences of life without the possibility of parole are unconstitutional for juvenile offenders.[58]

State laws regarding the practice of closed adoption may also require overhaul in light of the Convention's position that children have a right to identity from birth.

During his 2008 campaign for President, Senator Barack Obama described the failure to ratify the Convention as "embarrassing" and promised to review the issue[59] but he never did. No President of the United States has submitted the treaty to the United States Senate requesting its advice and consent to ratification since the US signed it in 1995.[60]

The United States has ratified two of the optional protocols to the Convention, the Optional Protocol on the Involvement of Children in Armed Conflict, and the Optional Protocol on the Sale of Children, Child Prostitution and Child Pornography.

Optional protocols

Two optional protocols were adopted by the UN General Assembly. The first, the Optional Protocol on the Involvement of Children in Armed Conflict requires parties to ensure that children under the age of 18 are not recruited compulsorily into their armed forces, and calls on governments to do everything feasible to ensure that members of their armed forces who are under 18 years do not take part in hostilities. This protocol entered into force on 12 July 2002.[61] As of 18 October 2018, 167 states are party to the protocol and another 14 states have signed but not ratified it.

The second, the Optional Protocol on the Sale of Children, Child Prostitution and Child Pornography, requires parties to prohibit the sale of children, child prostitution and child pornography. It entered into force on 18 January 2002.[62] As of 18 October 2018, 173 states are party to the protocol and another 9 states have signed but not ratified it.

A third, the Optional Protocol to the Convention on the Rights of the Child on a Communications Procedure, which would allow children or their representatives to file individual complaints for violation of the rights of children, was adopted in December 2011 and opened for signature on 28 February 2012. The protocol currently has 51 signatures and 45 ratifications: it entered into force on 14 April 2014 following the tenth ratification three months beforehand.

External links

Wikisourcehas original text related to this article:
UN Convention on the Rights of the Child

- United Nations General Assembly (20 November 1989). "Text of the UN Convention on the Rights of the Child"[63]. *ohchr.org*. UN Office of the High Commissioner for Human Rights. Retrieved 20 January 2015.<templatestyles src="Module:Citation/CS1/styles.css"></templatestyles>
- Signatures and ratifications[64], at depositary
- UNICEF web site[65]
- Procedural history, related documents and photos[66] on the *Convention on the Rights of the Child (with protocols)* in the Historic Archives of the United Nations Audiovisual Library of International Law[67]
- NGO Alternative Reports[68] submitted to the Committee on the Rights of the Child.
- Biography of Eglantyne Jebb, author of the original Declaration[69]
- Section related to the CRC on the Children's Rights Portal[70]
- "everychild.ca"[71] Child Rights Public Awareness Campaign of British Columbia, Canada. Resources include links and publications related to the Convention on the Rights of the Child.

Free Children from War conference

Part of a series on
Child soldiers
Main articles
• Child soldiers • History of child soldiers • Impact • Rehabilitation and reintegration
Issues
• Child abduction • Child sexual abuse • Forced marriage • Forced prostitution • Post traumatic stress disorder
Instances (examples)
• World War II • Africa • Central African Republic • Democratic Republic of Congo • India • Myanmar • Sierra Leone • Somalia • Sri Lanka
Legal aspects
• Paris Principles • Convention on the Rights of the Child • Optional protocol
Movement to end the use of child soldiers
• Red Hand Day
• v • t • e[72]

The **Free Children from War Conference** was a conference co-hosted by the French government and UNICEF on 5–6 February 2007 in Paris, France. The goal of the conference was to bring together countries, non-governmental organizations, and international organizations to discuss the issue of child soldiers . The 59 involved countries signed the Paris Principles and Paris Commitments, which update the Cape Town Principles and outline a practical approach to preventing the use of child soldiers and the reintegration of current child soldiers.[73] The Principles define a child associated with an armed force or armed group as:

... any person below 18 years of age who is or who has been recruited or used by an armed force or armed group in any capacity, including but not limited to children, boys and girls, used as fighters, cooks, porters, messengers, spies or for sexual purposes. It does not only refer to a child who is taking or has taken a direct part in hostilities. (p. 7).

Attendees

59 countries attended the conference: Afghanistan, Austria, Belgium, Benin, Brazil, Bulgaria, Burundi, Cambodia, Canada, Chad, China, Colombia, Côte d'Ivoire, Cyprus, Czech Republic, Democratic Republic of Congo, Denmark, Estonia, Finland, France, Germany, Ghana, Greece, Haiti, Hungary, Indonesia, Ireland, Italy, Japan, Liberia, Lithuania, Luxembourg, Mali, Malta, Monaco, Nepal, Netherlands, Niger, Norway, Peru, Poland, Portugal, Qatar, Republic of Congo, Romania, Russia, Sierra Leone, Slovakia, Slovenia, Somalia, South Africa, Spain, Sri Lanka, Sudan, Sweden, Switzerland, Timor, Uganda, and the United Kingdom.[74]

External links

- Full text of the Paris Commitments[75]
- Full text of the Paris Principles[76]
- Child Soldiers International[77]

Optional Protocol on the Involvement of Children in Armed Conflict

Optional Protocol to the Convention on the Rights of the Child on the Involvement of Children in Armed Conflict

Signed	25 May 2000
Location	New York
Effective	12 February 2002
Condition	10 ratifications
Signatories	130
Parties	168
Depositary	UN Secretary-General
Languages	Arabic, Chinese, English, French, Russian and Spanish

🌐 Optional Protocol to the Convention on the Rights of the Child on the Involvement of Children in armed conflict at Wikisource

Part of a series on
Child soldiers
Main articles

- Child soldiers
- History of child soldiers
- Impact
- Rehabilitation and reintegration

Issues

- Child abduction
- Child sexual abuse
- Forced marriage
- Forced prostitution
- Post traumatic stress disorder

Instances (examples)

- World War II
- Africa
- Central African Republic
- Democratic Republic of Congo
- India
- Myanmar
- Sierra Leone
- Somalia
- Sri Lanka

Legal aspects
• Paris Principles • Convention on the Rights of the Child • Optional protocol
Movement to end the use of child soldiers
• Red Hand Day
• <u>v</u> • <u>t</u> • <u>e</u>[78]

The **Optional Protocol to the Convention on the Rights of the Child on the Involvement of Children in Armed Conflict** (OPAC), also known as the child soldier treaty, is a multilateral treaty whereby states agree to: 1) prohibit the conscription into the military of children under the age of 18; 2) ensure that military recruits are no younger than 16; and 3) prevent recruits aged 16 or 17 from taking a direct part in hostilities. The treaty also forbids non-state armed groups from recruiting anyone under the age of 18 for any purpose.

The United Nations General Assembly adopted the treaty as a supplementary protocol to the Convention on the Rights of the Child by resolution 54/263 on 25 May 2000. The protocol came into force on 12 February 2002.

As of September 2018, 168 states are party to the protocol and a further 13 states have signed but not ratified it.

Background

The Convention on the Rights of the Child (1989) defines a child as any person under the age of 18.

Throughout history and in many cultures, children have been extensively involved in military campaigns. In World War I, in Great Britain 250,000 boys under 18 managed to join the army. In World War II, child soldiers fought throughout Europe, in the Warsaw Uprising,[79] in the Jewish resistance, and in the Soviet Army. After the Cold War ended, the number of armed conflicts grew and the use of children for military purposes surged, affecting as many as 300,000 children worldwide annually by the end of the 1990s.

Progress towards ending the use of children for military purposes has been slow, partly because many national armed forces have relied on children to fill their ranks. Initial efforts to limit the participation of children in armed conflict began with the adoption of the Additional Protocols to the 1949 Geneva Conventions, adopted in 1977 (Art. 77.2). The new Protocols prohibited the military recruitment of children aged under 15 and their direct participation in hostilities, but continued to allow state armed forces and non-state armed groups to recruit children from age 15 and use them in warfare.[80] In addition, the Protocols did not prohibit belligerents from using children younger than 15 in hostilities when their participation was not "direct"; for example, as scouts, porters, informants, spies, message-carriers and in other support roles.

When the same limited standards were incorporated into the Convention on the Rights of the Child (CRC) in 1989, children's rights advocates were left frustrated, believing that a treaty establishing the fundamental rights of children ought to protect them from all forms of military involvement. To achieve this, a small group of human rights campaigners and sympathetic governments began a global campaign for a new treaty, which was adopted in 2000 as the Optional Protocol to the Convention on the Rights of the Child on the involvement of children in armed conflict (OPAC).

The campaign for a new treaty

Initial negotiations

By 1994, five years after the Convention on the Rights of the Child was adopted, children's rights advocates and sympathetic governments had persuaded the international community to establish a working group of the United Nations Commission on Human Rights. Its mandate was to begin negotiations on a new protocol to the Convention that would raise standards regarding the use of children for military purposes.

While the large majority of states negotiating the protocol were willing to end all military recruitment of children under the age of 18 (the so-called "straight-18" principle), a small number were opposed: Bangladesh, Cuba, Israel, South Korea, Kuwait, Pakistan, the United Kingdom (UK) and the United States (US). According to Jo Becker, a human rights advocate actively involved in the negotiations:

> Governments began a series of annual negotiations in Geneva, but by 1998, negotiations floundered as it became clear that governments that had long used under-eighteens in their national armed forces, notably the United States and United Kingdom, were not willing to support a new standard that conflicted with their national practice.

While some of the states opposed to the change said nevertheless that they would not block it, the US insisted on its position, according to Becker.

Instrumental in gathering high-level support for the treaty was a proposal by children's rights advocates for a major study on the effect of armed conflict on children. The study was proposed by the Committee on the Rights of the Child, commissioned by the UN General Assembly, and produced by Graça

Machel in 1996: *Impact of armed conflict on children*. The report was particularly concerned with the use of younger children as participants in armed conflict, presenting evidence that many thousands of children were being killed, maimed, and psychiatrically injured around the world every year. It also called for an end to the recruitment of children by all armed forces.

The Coalition to Stop the Use of Child Soldiers

As negotiations on the new treaty stalled in 1998, the Coalition to Stop the Use of Child Soldiers (now known as Child Soldiers International) was established by six human rights and humanitarian organizations (Amnesty International, Human Rights Watch, International Federation Terre des Hommes, Jesuit Refugee Service, the Quaker United Nations Office (Geneva) and Save the Children). With the goal of incorporating the straight-18 principle into the new treaty, the Coalition quickly seeded national affiliates in more than thirty countries. The Coalition worked in alliance with a small group of states actively advocating for the straight-18 principle internationally: Canada, Denmark, Ethiopia, Finland, Japan, Mozambique, Norway, Portugal, South Africa, Sweden, and Switzerland.

With initial funding from the Canadian government, the Coalition organised a series of intergovernmental regional conferences; the African and Latin-American conferences strongly supported the straight-18 principle. The European conference supported an end to the participation of children in armed conflict, but not their recruitment, due to opposition from Austria, France, Germany, Luxembourg, the Netherlands and the UK, which were all recruiting children aged 16 or 17 into their own armed forces. (As of 2017, all except Luxembourg were still doing so.)

By 1999, the straight-18 principle enjoyed the support of the large majority of states, as well as the Committee on the Rights of the Child, the International Committee of the Red Cross, the International Labour Organization, the European Parliament, the Organization of African Unity, and the World Council of Churches.

Final negotiations

In the final negotiations, only five states still advocated against the straight-18 principle: Egypt, Kuwait, Singapore, the UK and, most trenchantly, the US. The US, with British support, continued to insist that it would not support a treaty that prevented it from sending 17 year-olds into battle. According to Becker, the US relented following an intervention from Secretary of State Madeleine Albright, although the US and UK continued to insist on their right to recruit children from age 16 (UK) and 17 (US).

This change allowed a compromise consensus between the negotiating parties, in which the new treaty would not prevent states from recruiting children into their armed forces from age 16 or 17, but would require that "all feasible measures" be taken to ensure that children did not participate "directly" in hostilities.

Extent of ratification and the straight-18 position

The OPAC treaty has been widely ratified. As of February 2018, 167 states had ratified or acceded to the treaty; a further 13 states had signed but not yet ratified it.

In addition, following OPAC's adoption the number of states restricting enlistment to adults aged over 18 has increased substantially, according to Child Soldiers International: from 83 in 2001 to 126 in 2016, which is 71 percent of countries with armed forces. These include several states where child recruitment had been routine, including Colombia and Sierra Leone. Approximately 60 non-state armed groups have also entered agreements to stop or scale back their use of children.

Despite this trend, Child Soldiers International reports that the recruitment of children for military purposes remains widespread, including by armed forces in the three most populous countries – China, India and the United States – and the most economically powerful (all G7 countries apart from Italy and Japan). A large number of non-state armed groups also recruit and use children routinely, especially following a recent surge in child recruitment by militant Islamist movements in Africa and the Middle East, as well as by militias opposing them.

'OPAC turns 18': 18th Anniversary event, 2018

On 21 February 2018 a meeting was held at the UN to mark the treaty's 18th anniversary. The meeting, co-sponsored by Child Soldiers International, UNICEF, and the governments of Belgium, Canada, Colombia, France and Sierra Leone, was attended by approximately 100 delegates. The Special Representative of the UN Secretary-General for Children and Armed Conflict, Virginia Gamba, reported on the progress made and still to be achieved since the treaty was adopted:

> We have really come a long way. Today, 18 years later, we should celebrate the quantifiable progress accomplished. The issue of children and armed conflict has been squarely placed on the international peace and security agenda. Since 2000, at least 130,000 child soldiers were released due to the collective efforts of child protection actors. Thousands more were spared the ordeal of recruitment and use – because their country

has joined OPAC and put in place measures to protect them. Making sure all boys and girls released and their communities have access to meaningful reintegration – to help them overcome the harrowing experiences they have been through – is essential. But this remains a huge challenge.

Provisions of the OPAC treaty

Main obligations

The main obligations of the OPAC treaty are as follows:

- No state party may recruit any person who has yet to attain a minimum age specified by the state (in a binding declaration deposited with the UN on ratification), and in all cases the minimum age must not be lower than 16 years.
- States parties whose armed forces recruit children aged 16 or 17 must:
  - not compel children to join their armed forces;
  - ensure that "reliable proof of age" is provided before enlistment;
  - ensure prior to enlistment that child applicants are "fully informed" of the duties of military service, that their choice to enlist is "genuinely voluntary", and that their parents or legal guardians give their "informed consent"; and
  - "take all feasible measures" to ensure that child recruits do not take part directly in hostilities;
- Non-state armed groups "should not, under any circumstances, recruit or use in hostilities" any child under the age of 18 (the legal force of this is uncertain, however).
- States parties to the treaty must report periodically on its implementation to the Committee on the Rights of the Child.

Other provisions

Other provisions of the treaty include the following:

- States parties must cooperate with each other in the implementation of the treaty and support financially and technically "in the rehabilitation and social reintegration" of persons who were recruited unlawfully as children.
- Any state can leave the treaty at a year's notice, but not if engaged in armed conflict at the time.
- The treaty does not prevent states from operating military schools, which are common in many countries, provided that these comply with the legal requirements governing education in the Convention on the Rights of the Child.

- The treaty allows states the option of raising their minimum enlistment age at any point and depositing an updated binding declaration to that effect with the United Nations; any state doing so is then bound by the revised minimum age and may not lower it.

Commentary of the International Committee of the Red Cross

The sentence "States Parties shall take all feasible measures to ensure that members of their armed forces who have not attained the age of 18 years do not take a direct part in hostilities" was adapted from Article 77.2 of the Additional Protocol I to the Geneva Conventions of 12 August 1949, and relating to the Protection of Victims of International Armed Conflicts, adopted in 1977, with an alteration from fifteen years to eighteen years and some other minor modifications. ("The Parties to the conflict shall take all feasible measures in order that children who have not attained the age of fifteen years do not take a direct part in hostilities and, in particular, they shall refrain from recruiting them into their armed forces.")

The ICRC commentary on Protocol I makes clear that it does not require a complete ban on the use of children in conflict. The ICRC had proposed that the Protocol require parties to "take all *necessary* measures" but final text uses the wording "take all *feasible* measures" which is not a total prohibition on their doing so. Furthermore, refraining from recruiting children under fifteen does not exclude children who volunteer for armed service. During the negotiations over the clause "take a part in hostilities," the word "direct" was added, opening up the possibility that child volunteers could be involved indirectly in hostilities, gathering and transmitting military information, helping in the transportation of arms and munitions, provision of supplies, etc.

National responses

Australia

The Australian Defence Force Cadets follows the Optional Protocol to the Convention on the Rights of the Child on the Involvement of Children in Armed Conflict but still accepts cadets between the ages of 13–18 (except staff) and sometimes brings them onto ADF bases.

United Kingdom

As noted above, at the time of OPAC's negotiation, the UK joined the US in actively resisting the majority view of negotiating states that 18 should be the minimum age for all forms of military recruitment. Then, as now, the UK permits its armed forces to enlist from age 16, and allows children to apply aged 15 years, 7 months.

On ratification of the treaty, the UK's binding declaration stated its understanding that, while it would endeavour not to use child recruits in hostilities, the protocol "...would not exclude the deployment of members of its armed forces under the age of 18 to take a direct part in hostilities where: a) there is a genuine military need to deploy their unit or ship to an area in which hostilities are taking place; and b) by reason of the nature and urgency of the situation:- i) it is not practicable to withdraw such persons before deployment; or ii) to do so would undermine the operational effectiveness of their ship or unit, and thereby put at risk the successful completion of the military mission and/or the safety of other personnel."

According to Child Soldiers International, the UK deployed 22 armed forces personnel aged under 18 to Iraq and Afghanistan between 2003 and 2010. The Committee on the Rights of the Child has urged the UK to alter its policy so as to ensure that children cannot take part in hostilities under any circumstances.

External links

- The full text of this treaty[81]
- List of ratifications[82]
- Guide to the Optional Protocol on the involvement of children in armed conflict[83] UNICEF, Coalition to Stop the Use of Child Soldiers, 2003

Rehabilitation and reintegration of child soldiers

Part of a series on
Child soldiers
Main articles
• Child soldiers • History of child soldiers • Impact • Rehabilitation and reintegration
Issues
• Child abduction • Child sexual abuse • Forced marriage • Forced prostitution • Post traumatic stress disorder
Instances (examples)
• World War II • Africa • Central African Republic • Democratic Republic of Congo • India • Myanmar • Sierra Leone • Somalia • Sri Lanka
Legal aspects
• Paris Principles • Convention on the Rights of the Child • Optional protocol
Movement to end the use of child soldiers
• Red Hand Day
• $\underline{v}$ • $\underline{t}$ • $\underline{e}$[84]

Figure 14: *A group of demobilised child soldiers in the DRC*

Part of a series on
War
• $\underline{v}$ • $\underline{t}$ • $\underline{e}^{85}$

Part of a series on
Slavery

- v
- t
- e[86]

The **rehabilitation and reintegration of child soldiers** is defined by Child Soldiers International as:

> *The process through which children formerly associated with armed forces/groups are supported to return to civilian life and play a valued role in their families and communities*

A child soldier is "...any person below 18 years of age who is or who has been recruited or used by an armed force or armed group in any capacity".

Generally, reintegration efforts seek to return children to a safe environment, to create a sense of forgiveness on the behalf of the child's family and community through religious and cultural ceremonies and rituals, and encourage the reunification of the child with his or her family. Often the first step is to reunite the former child soldier with their family and provide adequate monetary and institutional support. Access to education is one of the most requested forms of support in post-conflict environments, but is often unavailable for economic reasons. Some studies have shown that community-led reintegration is more beneficial than Western-driven trauma healing in dealing with the psychological challenges of reintegration.

There is often a stigma that children who belonged to armed groups are immoral, untrustworthy, or dangerous and therefore many individuals are rejected by community members, making reintegration difficult. Reintegration efforts can become challenging when a child has committed war crimes, as in these cases stigma and resentment within the community can be exacerbated.

Female child soldiers commonly face additional barriers to successful reintegration. Girls report significantly higher rates of rape and sexual abuse during a conflict and are, therefore, confronted with unique, gender-specific challenges. They often face stronger stigmatisation on their return to the community since they are often considered tainted by sexual relationships that occurred outside of marriage. They are often ostracised upon return, ridiculed, verbally and physically attacked and prohibited from marrying.

Child soldiers

As defined by the Paris Principles, a child soldier is:

> *"...any person below 18 years of age who is or who has been recruited or used by an armed force or armed group in any capacity, including but not limited to children, boys and girls, used as fighters, cooks, porters, messengers, spies or for sexual purposes. The document is approved by the United Nations General Assembly. It does not only refer to a child who is taking or has taken a direct part in hostilities."*

Child soldiers can take on many roles, including active fighting, acting as spies or lookouts, or acting in support roles, such as medic, porter, cook, or agricultural labourer.[87] While some child soldiers are abducted and forced to serve, others choose to serve. In many countries choosing to serve in an armed group is the best alternative for the child. Many children join the military because these groups will provide food, shelter, and a sense of security. For instance, in the Democratic Republic of Congo, the choices facing children are often "to join the military, become a street child, or die" (Refugees International 2002). Similar situations face children throughout the world, with cited instances in Columbia and Sri Lanka. There is often a stigma that children who belonged to armed groups are immoral, untrustworthy, or dangerous and therefore many individuals are rejected by community members, making reintegration difficult. Former soldiers often have to fabricate "second stories" and live in fear of their former identity being discovered and it leading to loss of status, discrimination, exclusion, or even retaliation.There are also two areas of reintegration that warrant special consideration: female child soldiers and drug use among child soldiers.[88] Child soldiers under the influence of drugs or who have contracted sexually transmitted diseases require additional programming specific to their unique needs.

Reintegration

Child Soldiers International defines reintegration as:

> *'The process through which children formerly associated with armed forces/groups are supported to return to civilian life and play a valued role in their families and communities"*

To facilitate the disarmament, demobilisation, and reintegration of former members of armed groups, the United Nations introduced the Integrated DDR Standards in 2006.[2] Disarmament, demobilisation and reintegration (DDR) are applied strategies for executing successful peacekeeping operations, especially after civil wars. Disarmament entails the physical removal of the means of combat from ex-belligerents (weapons, ammunition, etc.), demobilisation entails the disbanding of armed groups, and reintegration describes the process of reintegrating former combatants into civilian society, reducing the possibility of a resurgence of armed conflict. DDR programmes usually have a number of components including a focus on psycho-social care, the return of ex-child soldiers to education, job training, and supporting local initiatives, usually through various regional partnerships). Such programmes usually aim for children to either go back to their families or be placed with foster families.

Programs that aim to rehabilitate and reintegrate child soldiers, such as those sponsored by UNICEF, often emphasise three components: family reunification/community network, psychological support, and education/economic opportunity.[89] These efforts take a minimum commitment of 3 to 5 years in order for programs to be successfully implemented. Generally, reintegration efforts seek to return children to a safe environment, to create a sense of forgiveness on the behalf of the child's family and community through religious and cultural ceremonies and rituals, and encourage the reunification of the child with his or her family.

Reintegration efforts can become challenging when a child has committed war crimes, as in these cases stigma and resentment within the community can be exacerbated. In situations such as these, it is important that the child's needs are balanced with a sense of community justice.[90] If such situations are not addressed children face an increased likelihood of re-enlistment.

Reintegration programme components

Family reunification

Often the first step in the reintegration of child soldiers is family unification, that is reuniting the former child soldier with their families and providing adequate monetary and institutional support. When this is not possible attempts can be made to place former child soldiers in foster families or to assist the former child soldier with independent living. In Angola a family reunification project was implemented entitled "self-building program" which supported former child soldiers and their families in constructing a house.[91] There may be concerns as to whether the family will accept the child after they have been

Figure 15: *A former Ugandan child soldier retrained as a bricklayer*

a soldier. In Uganda this acceptance was assisted through the use of cleansing ceremonies, which assisted in the removal of community stigmatisation by "decontaminating" the child.

Community support and acceptance

Community networks can also be instrumental in the reintegration of former child soldiers with their families and communities. Reintegration programs often aim to find a constructive social role for the former child soldier. Working in partnership with local NGOs can be important for capacity-building and to facilitate sustainable efforts that will last after international actors have left. In Angola a community-based network called Catechist has a partnership with approximately 200 churches. The Catechist was perceived as being neutral, having a sense of authority, and adherence to international humanitarian law. Given this, the network, respected by the community, has the capacity for outreach and was able to provide ongoing support the reintegration process. The broader community has also been witness to and a victim of the armed conflict. A focus on community healing is also an aspect of reintegration, because community healing can lead to community acceptance. Many armed conflicts occur among collectivistic societies and therefore this can be a better-suited approach. By involving the community in the healing processids outsider imposition of values and understanding. Before community healing can occur a more comprehensive approach is needed to remedy many systemic problems in war zones such as the short supply of water, food, shelter and other basic necessities. There is often a lack of professional, institutional, and economic support for this form of family and community reintegration.

Psychological support

As part of their training child soldiers undergo a process of asocialisation and, consequently, may be resistant to changing their identity from that of a child soldier. Studies have shown that psychosocial approaches, a psychological process that takes place in the community, are more beneficial than Western-driven trauma healing in dealing with the psychological aspects of reintegration. Some of these approaches encompass emotional expression, group and individual counselling, cultural rituals, social reconstruction and emotional reintegration. These psychosocial approaches support physical health as well as cognitive, emotional and moral development. Through partnerships with local NGOs clinical psychologists are often able to train locals to administer these interventions empowering the community more directly in the healing process, instead of silencing local healers and local practices. Given this reintegration programs emphasise the opportunity for former child soldiers to establish trusting and consistent relationships with adults and also emphasise a family-based environment. Traditional rituals and family and community mediation can help to address the antisocial and aggressive behaviour a child soldier may have developed, and help the child recover from stressful and traumatic experiences.

Education and economic opportunity

Education and economic opportunities help former child soldiers to establish new identities for themselves and to empower them to take active control of their lives. Access to education is one of the most requested forms of support in post-conflict environments. It is often unavailable for economic reasons. Access to formal education remains a challenge for a multitude of reasons as the need to earn an income can supersede the desire for education, families may not be able to afford education, schools are often destroyed in conflicts, teachers may have fled or have been killed, or there may be difficulty in obtaining documentation to enroll in educational institutions. In addition child soldiers frequently feel shame for their actions or there is resentment between the former child soldiers and their classmates. It is important to strike a balance between education and economic opportunities. Key aspects of striking this balance often include the creation of accelerated education programmes which suit the needs of the former child soldiers, focusing education on approaches that can generate income, such as market-appropriate vocational training and the inclusion of child soldier reintegration in the post-conflict economic policy of the country in question.

Female child soldiers

Girls report significantly higher rates of rape and sexual abuse during a conflict and are, therefore, confronted with unique, gender-specific challenges. They often face stronger stigmatisation on their return to the community since they are often considered tainted by sexual relationships that occurred outside of marriage. They are often ostracised upon return, ridiculed, verbally and physically attacked and prohibited from marrying.

Between 1990 and 2002, female soldiers were involved in internal armed conflicts in 36 countries. In countries such as Angola, El Salvador, Ethiopia, Sierra Leone, and Uganda as many as 40% of child soldiers were female. In Colombia many girls joined armed groups for ideological or financial reasons. Being in with love with an existing soldier is also a common reason cited. In Colombia and Cambodia girls are also often given as "tax payment" by parents. While serving as part of a fighting group is a traumatic experience for any child, the gender of the child must be taken into account in order to ensure that both males and females get effective help. Local anecdotes suggest that females are often referred to as "wives", "rewards for soldiers' valor", or victims of social terror. Other common roles include spies, porters, or minesweepers.

A 13-year-old fighter from Honduras reports:

> *Later I joined the armed struggle. I had all the inexperience and the fears of a little girl. I found out that girls were obliged to have sexual relations to alleviate the sadness of the combatants. And who alleviated our sadness after going with someone we hardly knew?*

Health and psycho-social effects after reintegration

Evidence has shown that female soldiers are released (as part of a DDR program) at lower rates than male soldiers.[1] Many female child soldiers suffer from a variety of health effects including pregnancy and birth complications, vaginal and cervical tearing and sores, and those relating to gender inequalities such as poorer health care, heavier workloads, and less freedom.[1] Other health effects include STDs and HIV which may be passed down during pregnancy, childbirth or breastfeeding. The consequences of pregnancies depend on the practices of the armed group concerned. Females could either be encouraged to carry the pregnancy, to create future fighters or be forced to abort. After childbirth female soldiers are often required to give their child to peasants to raise, to be reclaimed when he or she reaches fighting age.

During reintegration many female former child soldiers experience a variety of negative psycho-social effects. For example former Sierra Leonean female

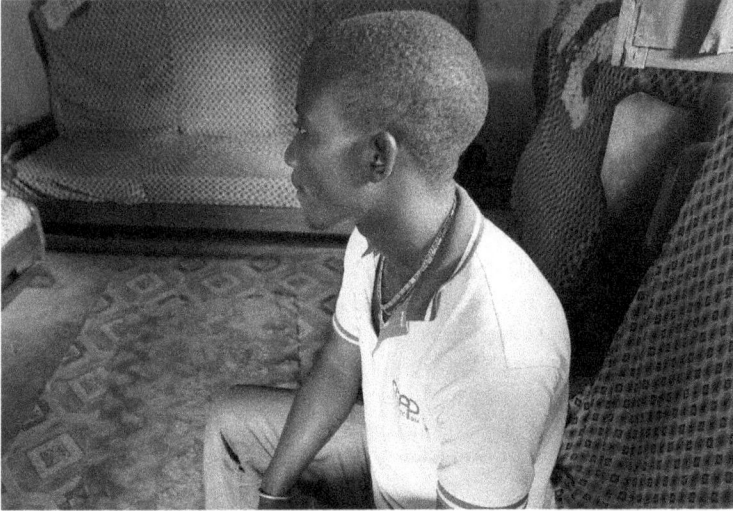

Figure 16: *This former DRC child soldier first picked up a gun when he was 12. Since demobilising, his community has largely welcomed him back.*

child soldiers were more likely to experience depression, anxiety, and lowered self-confidence than their male counterparts.[92] Reintegrated females often do not desire to enter into any marital relationships, sometimes choosing to withdraw from men altogether. This often results in further social stigma and increased societal isolation. Female child soldiers may be additionally stigmatised by their family or community for having had sexual relations and/or children out of marriage.[93] They may not want to participate in DDR programmes as this would draw attention to their association with an armed group.[94] DDR programs can also be too militarised to attract female enrolment; for example by failing to provide childcare, women's clothes or sanitary supplies.[95]

Case studies

Colombia

The Colombian armed conflict involves a number of groups including the Colombian government's National Army, guerilla groups (such as the National Liberation Army and the Revolutionary Armed Forces of Colombia), and paramilitary groups such as the United Self-Defense Forces of Colombia. In 2004 Colombia ranked fourth for the highest use of child soldiers in the world. As of 2012[96] there are about 5,000–14,000 children in armed groups in the country (Watchlist 2004, Watchlist 2012). Current DDR programs in

Colombia are carried out by the Colombian Family Welfare Institute (ICBF) and have focused on a post-conflict framework. Former Colombian child soldiers reported the most difficult parts of reintegration as being the transition from rural to urban life, reuniting with their families, and being removed from a context of organised armed violence.

Existing DDR programs in Colombia predominantly focus on protecting former soldiers from each other, rather than addressing the fear and stigma that each group suffers. Many in Colombia have viewed the services granted under DDR programmes as granting impunity to these individuals for former crimes. Instead, advocates have pushed for a public awareness through campaigns and advocacy in order to eliminate existing stigma (Thomas 2008).

Sierra Leone

Sierra Leone endured a civil war from 1991 to 2002. Child soldiers played a key role in the Revolutionary United Front and a lesser role in government forces and various militias. UNICEF states that during this period 84,666 children were officially documented as missing. The conflict seemed to come to an end with the signing of the Lome accord in 1999, but fighting did not cease until 2000. The disarmament and demobilisation portions ended in January 2002.

The rehabilitation and reintegration process focused primarily on community-based solutions. The main goal was to reunite children with their families. To this end a number of Interim Care Centers (ICCs) were established and administered by child protection NGOs. These ICCs sought to serve as temporary stops for children while their families was identified. 98% of demobilised children were reunited with one or both parents, older siblings or extended family. ICCs kept children for no longer than six weeks before returning them to family or foster care. ICCs began the process of rehabilitating former child soldiers into society. They separated them from the command structures that dominated much of their lives re-accustomed them to domestic life. This included performing chores, living to a normal schedule, receiving an education, and playing with other children. Notably, the ICCs were not focused on providing formal, western psychotherapy sessions and less than 100 children received therapy.

Reintegration centred on easing former child soldiers back into their communities. Parents and family members were often eager to welcome back children who had been child soldiers. To help them, various NGOs provided local family classes on how to deal with children who had been traumatised by the war. The local community, on the other hand, was less accepting of these children and often attacked aid workers for being associated with child soldiers. This did not apply to children who were part of the pro-government Civil Defense Force, which was widely seen as helpful by local communities. Wider social acceptance is shown in studies to have been crucial in easing trauma for child soldiers. To this end, communities were educated as to the traumas experienced by child soldiers as well as given help to organise traditional cleansing ceremonies. Additionally, children who were branded with symbols of the groups who abducted them were given plastic surgery to remove scars or tattoos. Beyond this, schools received additional funding in order to incentivise the intake of former child soldiers.

92% of the participants in UNICEF's formal DDR program were males. Former female child soldiers were often not included out of personal shame or due to not being combatants. Many female children were used for sex or married in bush weddings. These marriages tended to keep females isolated and their husbands would often not allow them to engage in rehabilitation programmes. ICCs were often separated by gender leading to female former child soldiers reporting instances of harassment or assault by males.

South Sudan

The Second Sudanese Civil War (1983–2002) was fought between the central Sudanese Government and the Sudan People's Liberation Army (SPLA). In 2005 a comprehensive peace agreement (CPA) was signed by both parties. The immediate release of all child soldiers was supposed to occur after the signing of the CPA, but this did not occur. Some, but not all, child soldiers were released from the SPLA. DDR policies were developed to help former soldiers and create a more stable infrastructure aimed at ensuring safety for the future. Creating the DDR policies was difficult because neither the government nor the SPLA shared the numbers or demographics of their soldiers.

Child soldiers were labelled a "special group" and in the drafting of the interim disarmament demobilisation and reintegration programme (IDDRP) they were given special protections. After the signing of the CPA policymakers began working on a multi-year DDR program. The DDR programmes included health checks, education opportunities, employment opportunities, bundles of supplies, and other services. After DDR began to be implemented it was discovered that most of the people who were being chosen to participate were not actually active members of the military. Therefore many of the people who had left the ranks of the military were being drawn back in order to take part in the DDR program. Largely the DDR efforts for child soldiers in South Sudan failed, mainly due to remaining tensions and a likelihood of continued war.

In 2013, the conflict resumed in South Sudan after the president and vice-president declared war on each other. As of March 2018[96] the war is still ongoing. In 2015 there were a reported 16,000 children being used by armed groups in South Sudan. Due to the armed conflict, in 2015 more than half of elementary- and primary-school-aged children were not receiving an education. Researchers have argued that education is vital in preventing re-recruitment, but accessing education is difficult for demobilised former child soldiers because of the effects of war, socioeconomic status, and a lack of educational structures. Children in South Sudan who have participated in or been involved with the conflict report feelings of isolation, stigma, and exclusion.

External links

- "Reintegration"[97], Child Soldiers International

Child Soldiers across the world

Child soldiers in Africa

Part of a series on
Child soldiers
Main articles
• Child soldiers
• History of child soldiers
• Impact
• Rehabilitation and reintegration
Issues
• Child abduction
• Child sexual abuse
• Forced marriage
• Forced prostitution
• Post traumatic stress disorder
Instances (examples)
• World War II
• Africa
• Central African Republic
• Democratic Republic of Congo
• India
• Myanmar
• Sierra Leone
• Somalia
• Sri Lanka
Legal aspects
• Paris Principles
• Convention on the Rights of the Child
• Optional protocol

Movement to end the use of child soldiers
• Red Hand Day
• v̲ • t̲ • e̲[98]

Child Soldiers in Africa refers to the military use of children under the age of 18 by national armed forces or other armed groups in Africa. Typically, this classification includes children serving in non-combatant roles (such as cooks or messengers), as well as those serving in combatant roles. In 2008, it was estimated that 40 percent of child soldiers worldwide were in Africa, and that the use of child soldiers in armed conflict was increasing faster than any other continent. Additionally, average age of children recruited as soldiers appears to be decreasing.[99] As of 2017, the UN listed that seven out of fourteen countries recruiting and using child soldiers in state forces or armed groups were in Africa: Central African Republic, Democratic Republic of the Congo, Mali, Nigeria, Somalia, South Sudan, Sudan.

Overview

Continental estimates

Exact data on the number of child soldiers in Africa is not known, partly due to the inaccessibility of some regions. In addition, there are a high number of unregistered births in several African nations, making it difficult to estimate the number of child soldiers in certain countries.

In 2003, the UN Office for the Coordination of Humanitarian Affairs estimated that up to half of children involved with state armed forces and non-state armed groups worldwide were in Africa. In 2004, Child Soldiers International estimated that 100,000 children were being used in this way on the continent;[100] in 2008, an academic estimate put the total at 120,000 children, or 40 percent of the global total of child soldiers.

Regions of concentration

Overall, incidences of child soldiers appear to be concentrated within Central and North Africa. The percentage of child soldiers as a proportion of all combatants ranges widely throughout conflicts in the continent from 0 percent to 53 percent.

In 2007, it was estimated that approximately 35,500 children were being used for military purposes in Africa's most intense conflicts in North Sudan/Darfur, South Sudan, Central African Republic and Nigeria. According to the UN,

Figure 17: *Military escort with rifle during trip*

in 2016 children were being used by armed groups in seven African countries (Central African Republic, Democratic Republic of the Congo, Mali, Nigeria, Somalia, South Sudan, Sudan) and by state armed forces in three (Somalia, Sudan, South Sudan). Below are some of the statistics related to the recruitment of child soldiers in various African nations:

Country	Child Soldiers Recruited	Since
North Sudan/Darfur	6,500	2003
South Sudan	17,000	2013
Central African Republic	10,000	2013
Nigeria and Neighboring Countries	2,000	2016 alone

Reasons for recruitment by armed groups

Child soldiers are typically recruited because they are seen by armed groups as expendable and cheap to maintain. Other factors include the global proliferation of light automatic weapons, which children can easily handle; the relatively greater willingness of children to fight for non-monetary incentives such as honor, prestige, revenge and duty; and the greater psychological malleability of children relative to adults, which makes them easier to control, deceive and indoctrinate. Some leaders of armed groups have claimed that children, despite their underdevelopment, bring their own qualities as combatants to a fighting unit, being often remarkably fearless, agile and hardy. Journalist Jeffrey Gettleman suggests that the concentration of child soldiers in Africa is due to the shift among armed groups from being ideal-oriented to economically-driven. Additionally, countries like Sudan have shifted towards the use of child soldiers after the decolonization and independence from Europe in 1956. Countries were led into poverty, disease, war, and kidnapping, which in turn led to forced child labor.

Risk factors for recruitment

Risk factors for child soldiers include being separated from their family or home and living in an area of conflict, even if the conflict is not within the same nation. Simon Reich, a professor at Rutgers University, argues that one of the biggest determinants in the recruitment of child soldiers is the lack of protection for people living at refugee camps. Reich cites the mass displacement and breakdown of rule of law that refugees experience as factors that allow for the recruitment of child soldiers to occur in these camps, and adds that he has found 1,100 attacks on refugee camps in Africa over the course of 50 years. The majority of child soldiers are forcibly recruited either through abduction, conscription, coercion, or by being born into an armed group.

However, there are still child soldiers that join armed groups of their own volition. Children in countries led into poverty resort to joining warring groups that provide materials they would no otherwise have, such as three meals a day, clean clothes, and medical care. In a 2004 study of children in military organizations around the world, Rachel Brett and Irma Specht pointed to a complex of factors that incentivize joining an armed group, particularly:

- Background poverty including a lack of civilian education or employment opportunities;
- The cultural normalization of war;
- Seeking new friends;
- Revenge (for example, after seeing friends and relatives killed); and
- Expectations that a "warrior" role provides a rite of passage to maturity.

Many times the children recruited remain in the armed forces as they are forced into acts of violence against their own families to ensure they cannot go back to their communities. Other times, children are given drugs to alter their state of mind to facilitate the way their thoughts are shaped by people in command.

Manipulation tactics

Ishmael Beah gives his first hand account of his experience of being a child soldier in his book, A Long Way Gone, and the details are graphic. He explains the tactics of manipulation used to obtain and brainwash children, turning them into killing machines, which ultimately made it extremely difficult for them to leave and reintegrate into society. Children are stripped of their home and family, and filled with fear and uncertainty as they search for parts of their country that have not been affected by war in order to seek refuge. However, for young boys like Ishmael, they are not always greeted with open arms; in fact they are often chased away or captured. According to Ishmael war ruined the hospitable nature of his country and replaced it with fear and distrust making entire villages afraid of young boys who they believe to be spies. Removing children from their homes and separating them from their families makes it easier for armies to be recruit children because it makes them feel like they are part of a family again.[101] In addition to the loss of familiarity military commanders oftentimes force children to take drugs like amphetamines, crack cocaine, palm wine, brown-brown (cocaine mixed with gunpowder), marijuana and tranquilizers in order to disengage the child's actions from reality. Those who tried to refuse were beaten or killed, and according to Ishmael, taking the drugs made it easier for them to kill because it numbed them of any emotions. Once they were addicted to drugs they "would do just about anything that was ordered".Wikipedia:Citation needed

Manipulation plays a huge part in brainwashing children into becoming soldiers in fact, the military specifically targets children for this reason. According to an article by Vision, a child's underdeveloped ability to assess danger makes them the perfect candidate to take risk and difficult assignments that adults would normally refuse.Wikipedia:Citation needed Children are more impressionable than adults with a less developed sense of morals and values, making it easy for them to be shaped by a military official. Oftentimes commanders would use revenge as a tool to motivate children to kill. According to Ishmael Beah he was told by his commanders to "visualize the enemy, the rebels who killed your parents, your family, and those who are responsible for everything that has happened to you." Children are turned into killers through a brutal initiation process. New recruits are often forced to kill escapees or even members of their own to prove they are worthy of recruitment, if they refused or tried to deny they would also be killed. Cannibalism is practiced by certain groups, they force recruits to eat or drink the blood of their freshly killed victim with the explanation that "it will make you stronger".Wikipedia:Citation needed

Legal definitions and obligations

Definitions

The Convention on the Rights of the Child defines a child as any person under the age of 18. The Paris Principles, which have been approved by the United Nations General Assembly, define a child associated with an armed force or group as:

> ...*any person below 18 years of age who is or who has been recruited or used by an armed force or armed group in any capacity, including but not limited to children, boys and girls, used as fighters, cooks, porters, messengers, spies or for sexual purposes. It does not only refer to a child who is taking or has taken a direct part in hostilities.*

Obligations

All African states are bound by the Convention on the Rights of the Child, which requires the state to "take all feasible measures to ensure that persons who have not attained the age of 15 years do not take a direct part in hostilities". Most African states are also bound by the higher standards of the Optional protocol on the involvement of children in armed conflict, which requires governments to "take all feasible measures to ensure that persons below the age of 18 do not take a direct part in hostilities and that they are not compulsorily recruited into their armed forces".

Trends

While the majority of African states have set the minimum age of recruitment at 18 and others are actively considering the same, in countries that have had a history of child soldiers, such as Angola, the government has pushed to lower the minimum age to 17. Such cases are legal given that the international law sets the minimum age at 15. Given the age which international law has set, countries like Burundi and Rwanda do have their minimum age of recruitment set at 15. Additionally, in times of war and need, Mozambique reserves the right to lower their minimum age of conscription to below 18.

Overview by country

Algeria: Children and youth have been involved in the violence in Algeria, participating among armed groups with and without links to the Algerian government. The establishment of Legitimate Defense Groups, which were essentially private militias, in 1997 furthered the use of child soldiers, since these groups are not required to report on their activity, and the government had little control over them.

Angola: Though the government of Angola denies the use of child soldiers, NGOs confirm that child soldiers are involved in both state forces and the National Union for the Total Independence of Angola (UNITA), and later on in the Front for the Liberation of the Cabinda Enclave. The practice of *rusgas*, forcible recruitment of youth, was practiced well into the 90s. The government estimated in 2003 that 10% of the armed fighters had been under 18; however it is suspected that the number is much higher. Child refugees in Namibia are believed to have been recruited to serve in the civil war. As of March 2004, an estimated 16,000 child soldiers needed to be demobilized in Angola, though the civil war ended in April 2002. Child soldiers in Angola were excluded from assistance in demobilizing because the government did not classify them as soldiers. Those who had been child soldiers during the war were excused from compulsory military service but could still serve on a voluntary basis; indeed, some children who had come of age while in the armed forces chose to stay in the military.

Benin: There is no evidence of the enlistment of child soldiers in Benin.

Botswana: There is no evidence of the enlistment of child soldiers in Botswana; however there is not a formal age qualification for service.

Burkina Faso: Child refugees in Burkina Faso have reportedly been recruited by armed groups in Sierra Leone and Liberia in the early 2000s. However, there is no evidence of child soldier recruitment by armed groups within Burkina Faso.

Burundi: Children as young as 8 years old were regularly recruited into Burundi's army, typically to serve as *doria*, a term meaning "ear agent" in Kirundi. These soldiers were used to collect information for the army. Those that were not recruited to be *doria* joined the Peace Guards, a government militia unit, or worse, risked being coerced or bribed to be informants for the opposition. Furthermore, 94 percent of child soldiers were not paid for their service. Recruitment of child soldiers escalated during peace processes as armed groups tried to strengthen themselves prior to negotiations. Children from Burundi were also recruited to fight in the conflict within the Democratic Republic of Congo. When detained, children who were suspected of being involved with armed groups may be tortured and held for long periods of time.

Cape Verde: There is no evidence concerning child soldiers in Cape Verde. The Coalition to stop the Use of Child Soldiers points out that the high number of unregistered births may be a challenge in determining the use of child soldiers in Cape Verde.

Cameroon: Though there is no evidence of the use of child soldiers in Cameroon, the country is home to refugees from neighboring war-torn countries such as Chad and Central African Republic, where many child refugees and former child soldiers have received social services from NGOs. There have been unconfirmed reports of kidnappings by armed groups in neighboring countries to recruit child soldiers. Furthermore, the high number of refugees meant that some births were not accompanied by legal records, further exacerbating concerns about trafficking of unregistered children for the sake of army recruitment.

Central African Republic: As many as 10,000 children were used by armed groups in the armed conflict in the Central African Republic (CAR) between 2012 and 2015, and as of 2016 the problem persists. The mainly Muslim "Séléka" coalition of armed groups and the predominantly Christian, "Anti-Balaka" militias have both used children in this way; some were as young as eight.

Several high-profile cases of child soldier recruitment into government forces occurred, which contradicted governmental claims of no child soldier recruitment. These child soldiers, though few in number, sometimes attained higher ranks after their service, but were accused of perpetrating human rights abuses and looting.

Although the majority of child soldiers in CAR have been demobilized as a result of the peace process, many remain involved with armed groups; poor access to education and jobs leave children with few alternatives to being soldiers.

In 2016, a measure of stability returned to CAR and, according to the United Nations, 2,691 boys and 1,206 girls were officially separated from armed groups. Despite this, the recruitment and use of children for military purposes increased by approximately 50 percent, mostly attributed to the Lord's Resistance Army.

The UN estimated in 2014 that up to 6,000 children were involved in the ongoing civil war, with all parties to the conflict recruiting children.[102]

Chad: Governmental turmoil for the past several decades has further increased Chad's susceptibility to armed conflict, reducing the population of war-ready individuals. As a result, children have been used as soldiers within Chadian forces as well as other armed groups both within Chad and neighboring Sudan.

Since 2007, more than 800 children have been demobilized in Chad. By 2017, Chad was considered by the United Nations to have put in place the necessary framework to end the use of child soldiers.

Comoros: There was no large-scale recruitment of child soldiers except for in one isolated conflict. In this conflict, children were recruited by armed groups that sought to secede from the state in 1997, however there is no evidence that the state forces used child soldiers. Support from the World Bank and UNDP helped reintegrate these child soldiers at the end of the crisis.

Democratic Republic of Congo: From 1996 the former president Laurent Kabila used children widely for military purposes.[103] During the first and second civil conflicts, all sides involved in the war actively recruited or conscripted child soldiers, known locally as *kadogos*, a Swahili term meaning "little ones".[104] There were many human rights violations committed by all sides in the conflict.

Even after demobilization efforts had begun, the initiative was not taken seriously and armed groups continued to use child combatants in addition to committing violations against women and girls including violence and trafficking.

The use of child soldiers in the Democratic Republic of Congo has been described as "endemic" by United Nations Organization Stabilization Mission in the Democratic Republic of the Congo (MONUSCO),[105] and in 2011 it was estimated that there were 30,000 children currently being used in combat.[106]

Republic of Congo: Child soldiers were used in both government and Ninja militia forces and were recruited, according to some sources, with bribes. The Ninjas, a branch of Ninja militia actively recruited child soldiers. By early 2004, 2,000 child soldiers that had been involved with the Ninja militia had registered for demobilization.

Côte d'Ivoire: Armed groups in Sierra Leone and Liberia reportedly recruited child refugees in Côte d'Ivoire in the early 2000s. Civil war erupted in late 2002, and both governmental and non-governmental forces recruited child soldiers. Apart from recruitment into child combat, children were also sexually trafficked.

Djibouti: The incidence of child soldiers in Djibouti in modern history was reported by Stolwijk and Horeman to be tied to the Front for the Restoration of Unity and Democracy (FRUD), formed in 1991.[107] This group signed a peace treaty with the government in 2001, though violence briefly resurged in 2014.[108]

Egypt: Data suggests that child soldiers are not currently employed in Egypt; however it has been noted that they are utilized to conduct terror attacks.

Equatorial Guinea: Data suggests that child soldiers are not currently employed in Equatorial Guinea, as there is no ongoing conflict in that state.

Eritrea: Though Eritrea has been known to use child soldiers in the past, it is unclear whether child soldiers are currently being used by the country's armed forces. This is especially hard to track given inconsistent and incomplete birth records.

Ethiopia: There is conflicting data on recent instances of child soldiers in Ethiopia. Though the government claims that it is actively working against the employment of child soldiers by the army—even turning away underage recruits—there is some evidence that child soldiers were being forcibly recruited in the late 90's.

Gabon: There have been no reports of child soldiers in Gabon.

Gamibia: There have been no reports of child soldiers in Gambia.

Ghana: There have been no reports of child soldiers in Ghana.

Guinea: By early 2004, there remained approximately 2,000 child soldiers in Guinea that needed to be demobilized. Neighboring countries of Liberia and Sierra Leone pose a threat to the safety of refugees and civilians in Guinea, particularly children, while their conflicts were underway. In the early 2000s, armed groups in these countries reportedly recruited child refugees staying in Guinea.

Guinea-Bissau: Child soldiers are believed to have been involved in Guinea-Bissau's armed conflict up until it ended in 2002. Though some concerns about young recruits have risen among governmental and non-governmental forces, the number of child soldiers in Guinea Bissau currently appears to be quite low, despite the state's previous armed conflicts.

Kenya: There is no evidence of child soldiers employed in Kenya's armed forces or in other armed groups.

Lesotho: There is no evidence of child soldiers employed in Lesotho's armed forces or in other armed groups.

Liberia: All sides in the Liberian civil war used child soldiers extensively. The Small Boy's unit formed an integral part of Liberian rebel forces in both Liberia and Sierra Leone's civil wars; the unit was first designated by Charles Taylor. The boys were not provided with sustenance—they were expected to engage in "snake patrol," looting surrounding villages. Taylor and others were later tried before the Special Court for Sierra Leone because of his involvement in recruiting child soldiers, and the prevalence of child soldiers declined soon after he went out of power. Soldiers were frequently given valium before a battle, known as "bubbles" or "10-10." Lack of reintegration resources prompted child soldiers in Liberia to enroll in other armed groups, seeking some form of employment. By early 2004, about 21,000 child soldiers still needed to be demobilized.

Libya: It is obligatory to serve in the armed forces once each citizen reaches 18 years of age. However, children receive military training from the age of 14.

Madagascar: Madagascar reports no requirement for children under 18 to serve in their armed forces.

Malawi: There is no use of child soldiers in Malawi. The minimum age to enter armed forces, military school, or training camps is 18.

Mali: While there is no evidence of children being recruited to the armed forces. The minimum age of entry to a military school is 12 years of age.

Mauritania: There is left over tension from conflict with Senegal in 1989 and in 1991, Article 18(1) of the Constitution went into effect, stating that every citizen has the responsibility to protect their country. Thus, citizens are allowed to voluntarily join the armed forces at the age of 16.

Mauritius: While there is not official army in Mauritius, there are two paramilitary forces in which 18 is the minimum age of recruitment.

Morocco: Moroccan national legislation, Article 16 of the Constitution, states that citizens must be 18 years of age to be recruited into the armed forces. Citizens are more likely to volunteer in the armed forces if they originate from urban areas and have a higher quality education. There are four military schools that allow youth, including those under the age of 18, to join the armed forces with a national exam as long as they have achieved a high school diploma. All citizens enrolled then go through the same training process and are able to leave at any point in time.

There is a history of armed conflict with the Polisario Front, but there is no direct evidence of children participating in the armed conflict. The conflict has since ended after the UN peace plan in 1991.

Mozambique: Thousands of child soldiers were used in the past conflict between Frelimo and Renamo. There is no longer evidence of child soldiers in Mozambique.

Namibia: Namibian national legislation, Article 15-2 of the 1990 Constitution, does not allow for children, defined by the legislation as a citizen under 16 years-old, to be placed in a situation that would be deemed harmful to them. However, Namibian Defense Force Personnel Policies declare that in order to be recruited, a candidate must be between 18 and 25 years of age.

Past conflict shows no evidence of using or not using child soldiers.

Niger: There is no official national legislation listing recruitment requirements.

Nigeria: The minimum age to volunteer into the armed forces is 18 years of age.

Rwanda: National legislation states that volunteers may be recruited at the minimum age of 16, but exceptions may be made for recruits. Rwandan People's Army reported about 5,000 citizens below 18 years of age in the year 1994. That same year, the Ministry of Defence dedicated themselves to clear the armed forces of children. In 1996, the Ministry of defence claimed that all children had been demobilised from the army. However, in 1997 there were 2,134 documentations of children associated with the army and 725 children had an army number. In 1998, 2,893 children were detained as suspects of genocide. Some children were sent to the Gitagata Re-Education Centre for males below 14 years of age.

Senegal: Legislation states 18 years as the age to enroll in the army, however the age has risen to 19 years in practice but not in legislation.

Seychelles: As of 1998, there has been no evidence of militarization of children in Seychelles. Military service is performed on a voluntary basis, and can only be performed when one has fulfilled one year of National Youth Service, after reaching the age of 16.

Sierra Leone: Existing evidence indicates that children have been viewed by military commanders as more trusting than adults, due to the fact that they are less likely to break rules; and they are also more likely to show bravery and commitment to military conduct–including principles such as sexual abstinence and refraining from using drugs.

Common use of children in warfare was common for a period of time during the Sierra Leone Civil War; though sociopolitical circumstances in Sierra Leone have improved to an extent, and policies have improved in subsequence. In 1998, children under the age of 18 were not allowed to be recruited. In the case of Kamajor culture, becoming a soldier was also seen as part of one's initiation into adulthood; and the Kamajors would also provide shelter and food for children who were able to survive and escape from attacks by the Revolutionary United Front.

Somalia: The Convention of the Rights of the Child was signed by the Somalian government in October 2015, affirming efforts to formally protect the rights of children to keep them from entering the war zone. In the past, children have been incentivized through promises for monetary provisions to be given to their families, or promises to future education.

South Africa: Current laws dictate that individuals cannot be deployed into combat before they are of 18 years of age; though there may be exceptions in the case of an "emergency."

Sudan: As of January 2017, an estimated number of 335 children were reported to have been recruited amidst the affairs of the current ongoing conflict in (North) Sudan within the last five years. In Sudanese culture, adulthood is believed to reached as young as 11 years of age, but on average most people reach it at the age of 15.

Children have been used in the military for decades in Sudan. Many of these children are grateful for being taken into the military, for it provided them with protection and the opportunity to protect or avenge those close to them.

In 2015, it was that 15,000 to 16,000 children may have been involved in the South Sudanese Civil War–which is currently still ongoing. Daniel Bekele, Africa director at Human Rights Watch, observed that many people find that "there is no cost to [the] crime" of sending out children onto the battlefield, and that many commanders have never been held accountable for the crime of leading thousands of children within their military troops.

Swaziland: There is no existing literature on child soldiers in Swaziland. The minimum age for military recruitment is 18 years old.

Tanzania: There is no existing literature on child soldiers in Tanzania. Government jobs, higher education and vocational training schools–however, require military service from individuals.

Togo: There is no existing literature on child soldiers in Togo. There seem to be laws protecting children under the pretense that there is a minimum age requirement for military service in Togo (some sources say 18 years of age, while other sources say 20 years of age).

Tunisia: There is no existing literature on child soldiers in Tunisia. Current laws seem to protect the recruitment of children for military service.

Uganda: Over the past twenty years the rebel Lord's Resistance Army has abducted more than 30,000 boys and girls as soldiers or sex slaves. At the height of the LRA's activity, children made up approximately 90% of its personnel. As of 2018[109], children are no longer recruited by state- or non-state armed forces in Uganda.

Zambia: There is no existing literature on child soldiers in Zambia, though laws provide a way for entities to recruit children for military purposes provided that consent is given by their parents.

Zimbabwe: In 2003, the *Guardian* reported multiple human rights violations by the National Youth Service, a state-sponsored youth militia. Originally conceived as a patriotic youth organisation, it became a paramilitary group of youth aged between 10 and 30, and was used to suppress dissent in the country. The organisation was finally banned in January 2018.

Treatment of child soldiers post-conflict

Many humanitarian efforts are aimed towards improving the situations of war-zoned areas, where children are more likely to be sent into battle, most commonly involving the provision of food, water, medicine and construction materials. However, the concept of psychological trauma in former and current soldiers is a topic of inquiry that has only recently garnered attention—and the act of socializing children has been identified as a related topic of inquiry. As a result, there has been an increase in efforts aimed towards assisting children on the mental level, in addition to the efforts aimed towards physical needs.

The Human Rights Watch has lobbied for the reintegration and rehabilitation of child soldiers worldwide, with many successful efforts in policy changes over time. However, it stands to be the case that there are still organizations that deploy children for military purposes-most of which operate in ways that make them hard to identify.

Restorative vs. retributive justice

Retributive justice is characterized by the punishment of criminal offenders by means equal to their crime,[110] ideally preventing future offenses from occurring.[111] In other words, retributive justice is more typically exemplifying of the traditional justice system, where criminals are punished based on an "eye for an eye" principle, where imprisonment, and/or punishment that is equivalent to the crime committed, is imposed on the offender.

In contrast, restorative justice aims to rehabilitate individuals-and is more characteristic of the enlightenment period, where all available knowledge can be used to create an account of why a criminal offense occurred. In the case of militarized children, the identification of the most effective way to prevent future offenses from occurring involves identifying and examining all people and other influential factors involved in the murder of other people. In most cases, restorative justice efforts involve the displacement of blame from individuals onto the conditions that forced them to enter into combat in the first place (for example, environments where the lives of family and friends are constantly at-risk of death due to life-threatening circumstances, where the military servitude of a child can help sustain the lives of people). Most restorative justice efforts are carried out with the objective of reintegration into a local community.

Both kinds of practices are oriented towards the future well-being of people. However, the main difference between the two lies in the accountability of war crimes, in which minority-aged soldiers may be held fully or partially account-able and therefore imprisoned, or deemed as innocent through the personal-ization of crimes.

Being forced to become a soldier at an early age oftentimes results in changes in personality and mentality, as well as changes in physical appearance. Often-times, such changes are an inherent part of the initiation process for becoming a slave.

Reintegration efforts

Primarily, DDR programs ("DDR" standing for "Disarmament, Demobiliza-tion, Reinsertion and/or Reintegration) facilitate the reintegration of child sol-diers. People who are eligible for such programs include people who are asso-ciated with armed forces, regardless of gender or age-though specific criteria for eligibility varies from place to place. Organizations that sanction one or more DDR programs include intergovernmental organizations such as the UN, The World Bank, and Organisation for Economic Co-operation and Develop-ment (OECD), as well as governmental organizations, like the African Union Commission.[112,113,114,115]

There are many problems that have arisen in past-to-present efforts of reinte-gration. Former child soldiers are often subject to stereotypic beliefs, which can work in tandem with other factors, such as poverty, in giving former child soldiers a reason to return to the battlefield.[116] Individuals who are not as-sociated with any armed forces have pretended to be ex-combatants for the purpose of benefiting from assistance programs; screenings which test prac-tical military skills are conducted to mitigate the potential for the problem of people who are not eligible for organization-based assistance. Individuals who entered into combat when they were children oftentimes do not remember much from before they were soldiers, which hinders efforts to reunite families. Young female recruits, in particular, are often taken in as wives; which has its potential for gender-specific, psychological consequences as well.[117] Prob-lems such as these are compounded by difficulties in identifying strategies for meeting both immediate and long-term needs of ex-combatants, especially by the limitation of resources and access to education, which can be doubly com-pounded by political instability.

Children who survive combat face another set of obstacles when trying to reen-ter normal civilian life. While former soldiers were provided with resources like food, water, shelter, security, and family reunification, they still needed help processing their experience and reconnecting with their communities af-ter being separated for so long. Many communities view these children as rebels incapable of making the transition back into society, this doubt from the community caused many to get pulled back into the army. Organizations like UNICEF realized that child soldiers need mental help in addition to physical help to be able to reintegrate. Healing of traumatic experiences, emotional abuse, protection from re-recruitment, education and the gradual reintroduction into society all play key roles in the successful rehabilitation of child soldiers and even then the process is not easy.

The rehabilitation process normally includes drug withdrawal, psychological adjustment, and treatment for post traumatic stress disorder which causes a number of symptoms: nightmares, flashbacks, aggressiveness, hopelessness, guilt, anxiety, fear and social isolation. Treatment is practiced through games and activities that emphasize trust-building and opportunities to practice nonviolent conflict resolution. Drawing, storytelling, music and drama are often used as ways for the children to communicate and process their experiences.[118]

Reintegration programs often do not meet the needs of girls due to the fact that they are designed mainly for boys. Child Soldiers International is evaluating girls' reintegration programs in Democratic Republic of Congo, in order to better support their successful return to community life.

Sponsored programs

There are many efforts that currently oriented towards raising awareness in regards to the consequences of being involved in the military as a child, as well as preventing the recruitment of child soldiers. Many efforts are aimed at advocacy and research, as well as supporting former child soldiers in their educational pursuits.[119,120] UNICEF, for instance, seek to raise awareness by placing emphasis on the "association" with armed groups, for the term "child soldier" lacks the capacity to encapsulate the variety of potential roles that children can fulfill in military affairs.[121] Some organizations, such as War Child and UNICEF, aim to help children and parents resist the appeal of involvement with armed groups by spreading access to education and by raising awarenss on the benefits of education.[122] Musicians and writers, who have experienced what it is like to be a soldier as a child, have supported organizations in their efforts to end the use of child soldiers.[123]

Child Soldiers International has recently released The Child Soldiers World Index for public use, a resource that can be used for keeping up-to-date on things such as minimum age of conscription in countries and minimum voluntary enlistment age, as well as hyperlinks that can be used to travel to online websites that contain historical information on past military recruitment of children.[124]

Role of international actors

The role of international actors has been crucial in protecting children from recruitment into armed forces. The Additional Protocols to the four Geneva Conventions of 1949, added in 1977, state that 15 is the minimum age for serving in armed forces. In 1989 the United Nations passed the Convention on the Rights of the Child (CRC). Article 38 states that "state parties shall take all feasible measures to ensure that persons who have not attained the age of 15 years do not take a direct part in hostilities." In 1999 the African Charter on the Rights and Welfare of the Child came into force—the only regional treaty that addresses the issue of child soldiers. Children are defined as anyone below 18 years of age according to the charter.

The UN Security Council, specifically, has identified the recruitment or use of child soldiers as one of the council's "six grave violations." It has passed several resolutions regarding the use of child soldiers: 1261 (1999), 1314 (2000), 1379 (2001), 1460 (2003), 1539 (2004), 1612 (2005), 1882 (2009), 1998 (2011) and 2225 (2015). In 2002 the Optional Protocol on the Involvement of Children in Armed Conflict came into force which stipulates that state actors, "shall take all feasible measures to ensure that persons below the age of 18 do not take a direct part in hostilities and that they are not compulsorily recruited into their armed forces". Forty-eight African states have now ratified the Optional Protocol:

Participant	Signature	Ratification, Accession (a), Succession (d)
Algeria		May 6, 2009 a
Angola		October 11, 2007 (a)
Benin	February 22, 2001	January 31, 2005
Botswana	September 24, 2003	October 4, 2004
Burkina Faso	November 16, 2001	July 6, 2007
Burundi	November 13, 2001	June 24, 2008
Cabo Verde		May 10, 2002 (a)
Cameroon	October 5, 2001	February 4, 2013
Central African Republic	September 27, 2010	September 21, 2017
Chad	May 3, 2002	August 28, 2002
Congo		September 24, 2010 (a)
Côte d'Ivoire		March 12, 2012 (a)

Democratic Republic of the Congo	September 8, 2000	November 11, 2001
Djibouti	June 14, 2006	April 27, 2011
Egypt		February 6, 2007 (a)
Eritrea		February 16, 2005 (a)
Ethiopia	September 28, 2010	May 14, 2014
Gabon	September 8, 2000	September 21, 2010
Gambia	December 21, 2000	
Ghana	September 24, 2003	December 9, 2014
Guinea		April 8, 2016 (a)
Guinea-Bissau	8 Sep 2000	September 24, 2014
Kenya	8 Sep 2000	January 28, 2002
Lesotho	6 Sep 2000	September 24, 2003
Liberia	22 Sep 2004	
Libya		October 29, 2004 a
Malawi	September 7, 2000	September 21, 2010
Mali	September 8, 2000	May 16, 2002
Mauritius	November 11, 2001	February 12, 2009
Morocco	September 8, 2000	May 22, 2002
Mozambique		October 19, 2004 (a)
Namibia	September 8, 2000	April 16, 2002
Niger		March 13, 2012 (a)
Nigeria	September 8, 2000	September 25, 2012
Rwanda		April 23, 2002 (a)
Senegal	September 8, 2000	March 3, 2004
Seychelles	January 23, 2001	August 10, 2010
Sierra Leone	September 8, 2000	May 15, 2002
Somalia	September 16, 2005	
South Africa	February 8, 2002	September 24, 2009

Sudan	May 9, 2002	July 26, 2005
Swaziland		September 24, 2012 (a)
Togo	November 15, 2001	November 28, 2005
Tunisia	April 22, 2002	January 2, 2003
Uganda		May 6, 2002 (a)
United Republic of Tanzania		November 11, 2004 (a)
Zambia	September 29, 2008	
Zimbabwe		May 22, 2013 (a)

Also by 2004, Africa had become the first continent where recruiters of child soldiers faced the consequences of international law with indictments from the Special Court of Sierra Leone, and investigations into child soldier recruitment in Uganda and the Democratic Republic of Congo under the Rome Statute.

The United Nations launched a campaign in 2014 called "Children, Not Soldiers" to emphasize that children should not be involved in armed conflicts. This campaign was launched in 8 countries of concern, 5 of which were African nations: Chad, the Democratic Republic of the Congo, Somalia, South Sudan, and Sudan. The campaign was considered to be particularly successful in Chad, as well as South Sudan and Somalia; since its inception, the "Children, Not Soldiers" campaign has spread to other countries of concern.

Bibliography

<templatestyles src="Template:Refbegin/styles.css" />

- Drumbl, Mark A. (2012). *Reimagining Child Soldiers in International Law and Policy.* Oxford University Press. ISBN 978-0199592654.<templatestyles src="Module:Citation/CS1/styles.css"></templatestyles>
- Esack, Farid (2012). "Islam, children, and modernity A Qur'anic perspective". In Marcia J. Bunge. *Children, Adults, and Shared Responsibilities: Jewish, Christian and Muslim Perspectives.* Cambridge University Press. pp. 99–118. ISBN 978-1107011144.<templatestyles src="Module:Citation/CS1/styles.css"></templatestyles>
- "Child recruitment remains 'endemic' in DR Congo, UN says in new report"[125]. *United Nations.* 24 October 2013. Retrieved 5 April 2014.<templatestyles src="Module:Citation/CS1/styles.css"></templatestyles>

- Rakisits, Claude (2008). "Child Soldiers in the East of the Democratic Republic of the Congo"[126]. *Refugee Survey Quarterly*. **27** (4): 108–122. doi: 10.1093/rsq/hdn054[127]. Retrieved 5 April 2014.<templatestyles src="Module:Citation/CS1/styles.css"></templatestyles>
- Rosen, David M. (2012). *Child Soldiers: A Reference Handbook*. ABC-CLIO. ISBN 978-1598845266.<templatestyles src="Module:Citation/CS1/styles.css"></templatestyles>
- "Central African Republic: over 6,000 child soldiers may be involved in fighting, UN says"[128]. *United Nations*. 17 January 2014. Retrieved 9 April 2014.<templatestyles src="Module:Citation/CS1/styles.css"></templatestyles>

Further reading

<templatestyles src="Template:Refbegin/styles.css" />

- Vigh, Henrik (2006). *Navigating Terrains of War: Youth and Soldiering in Guinea-Bissau* (Repr. ed.). New York: Berghahn. ISBN 978-1-84545-148-6.<templatestyles src="Module:Citation/CS1/styles.css"></templatestyles>

Child soldiers in the Central African Republic

Part of a series on
Child soldiers
Main articles
• Child soldiers • History of child soldiers • Impact • Rehabilitation and reintegration
Issues
• Child abduction • Child sexual abuse • Forced marriage • Forced prostitution • Post traumatic stress disorder
Instances (examples)
• World War II • Africa • Central African Republic • Democratic Republic of Congo • India • Myanmar • Sierra Leone • Somalia • Sri Lanka
Legal aspects
• Paris Principles • Convention on the Rights of the Child • Optional protocol
Movement to end the use of child soldiers
• Red Hand Day
• $\underline{v}$ • $\underline{t}$ • $\underline{e}$[129]

As many as 10,000 children were used by armed groups in the armed conflict in the Central African Republic (CAR) between 2012 and 2015, and as of 2016 the problem persists natiowide. The mainly Muslim "Séléka" coalition of armed groups and the predominantly Christian, "Anti-Balaka" militias have both used children in this way; some are as young as eight.

Background

In 2005, armed conflict broke out between the government of President François Bozizé and armed groups, which had supported him to seize power in 2003. After peace talks brought some stability, conflict between the same parties erupted again in 2012. Armed groups formed the predominantly Muslim "Séléka" coalition, overthrowing the President.

In response to widespread human rights abuses perpetrated by the victorious Séléka, the "Anti-Balaka" emerged, a decentralised armed movement constituted mainly by Christian and animist militia, which had been supported by François Bozizé's government. This movement was then reinforced by defecting members of the armed forces loyal to the former president, and it began to commit abuses against the country's Muslim minority.

As sustained, nationwide violence between the two communities followed, both recruited children widely for military purposes. In 2013, UNICEF estimated that approximately 2,000 children were being used in this way, and that in 2015 the figure rose to between 6,000 and 10,000 children.

In May 2015, the *Forum de Bangui* brought together representatives of the transitional government, parliament, armed groups, civil society and religious leaders. At the meeting a number of armed groups signed an agreement on Disarmament, Demobilization, Reintegration and Repatriation (DDRR) and agreed to release thousands of children.

In 2016, a measure of stability returned to CAR and, according to the United Nations, 2,691 boys and 1,206 girls were officially separated from armed groups. Despite this, the recruitment and use of children for military purposes increased by approximately 50 per cent, mostly attributed to the armed group known as the Lord's Resistance Army.

Law

Definitions

The Convention on the Rights of the Child defines a child as any person under the age of 18. The Paris Principles, which have been approved by the United Nations General Assembly, define a child associated with an armed force or group as:

> "...any person below 18 years of age who is or who has been recruited or used by an armed force or armed group in any capacity, including but not limited to children, boys and girls, used as fighters, cooks, porters, messengers, spies or for sexual purposes. It does not only refer to a child who is taking or has taken a direct part in hostilities."

Obligations

Since 1992, CAR has been bound by the Convention on the Rights of the Child, which requires the state to "take all feasible measures to ensure that persons who have not attained the age of 15 years do not take a direct part in hostilities".

Since 2017, CAR has also been bound by the higher standards of the Optional protocol on the involvement of children in armed conflict, which requires the government to "take all feasible measures to ensure that persons below the age of 18 do not take a direct part in hostilities and that they are not compulsorily recruited into their armed forces."

Armed groups using children

According to Child Soldiers International, the main armed groups known to recruit children and use them in hostilities prior to 2012 were:

* Convention of Patriots for Justice and Peace (Convention des Patriotes pour la Justice et la Paix/CPJP).
* Democratic Front of the Central African People (Front Démocratique du Peuple Centrafricain/FDPC)
* Lord's Resistance Army (LRA)
* Movement of Central African Liberators for Justice (Mouvement des Libérateurs Centrafricains pour la Justice/MLCJ)
* People's Army for the Restoration of Democracy (Armée Populaire pour la Restauration de la Démocratie/APRD).
* Union of Democratic Forces for Unity (Union des Forces Démocratiques pour le Rassemblement/UFDR).

After 2012 the recruitment of children for military purposes saw a marked increase under the Séléka coalition and Anti-Balaka movement.

Risk factors

According to research in CAR by Child Soldiers International:

"Children have commonly joined armed groups of their own accord or at the behest of their families – this does not amount to voluntary recruitment, which requires free and informed consent. Children's primary motivations appear to include revenge after bereavement; the need for protection; and/ or a sense of duty to defend their communities. Poor access to education across the country has also been a contributing factor."

Military uses

According to Child Soldiers International, boys and girls as young as eight are trained to fight and use light weapons such as AK47s, knives and machetes, and are often used in frontline positions. Children are also widely used as guards, porters, messengers, spies, cooks, and for sexual purposes. The organization reports that youngest children are preferred for support tasks, such as preparing food, washing clothes, or acting as messengers and porters, and that a large number of children have been tasked with manning roadblocks and extorting money and valuables from travellers. The powerful stigma attached to sexual violence leads to substantial under-reporting, but the UN has received reports that a large number of girls and some boys were used for sexual purposes, including collective rape.

External links

- Child Soldiers International[130]
- UNICEF[131]

Child soldiers in the Democratic Republic of the Congo

Part of a series on
Child soldiers
Main articles
• Child soldiers • History of child soldiers • Impact • Rehabilitation and reintegration
Issues
• Child abduction • Child sexual abuse • Forced marriage • Forced prostitution • Post traumatic stress disorder
Instances (examples)
• World War II • Africa • Central African Republic • Democratic Republic of Congo • India • Myanmar • Sierra Leone • Somalia • Sri Lanka
Legal aspects
• Paris Principles • Convention on the Rights of the Child • Optional protocol
Movement to end the use of child soldiers
• Red Hand Day
• v • t • e[132]

During the first and second civil conflicts which took place in the Democratic Republic of the Congo (DRC), all sides involved in the war actively recruited or conscripted child soldiers, known locally as **Kadogos** which is a Swahili term meaning "little ones".[133] It has been estimated that the militia led by Thomas Lubanga Dyilo was 30 percent children. In 2011 it was estimated that 30,000 children were still operating with armed groups.[134] The United Nations

Organization Stabilization Mission in the Democratic Republic of the Congo (MONUSCO), released a report in 2013 which stated that between 1 January 2012 and 31 August 2013 up to 1,000 children had been recruited by armed groups, and described the recruitment of child soldiers as "endemic".[135]

The former president Laurent Kabila had used children in the conflict from 1996 onwards and it was estimated that up to 10,000 children, some aged only seven years old, served under him.[136]

The International Criminal Court (ICC), in the first trials held on human rights violations in the DRC, led to the first indictments, the first trials and the first convictions, in national jurisprudence for the use of children in combat.[137]

Background

It is estimated in the academic literature that up to 300,000 children form a part of both irregular, and regular armed forces worldwide, and that this number is increasing. In Africa it is estimated that up to 120,000 children, which is 40 percent of the worldwide total, are currently used as combatants or support personnel. Africa has the highest growth rate in the use of children in conflict, and on average, the age of those enlisted is also receding.[138] In 2003 it was estimated that up to 30,000 children were used as soldiers in the DRC, with children making up up to forty percent of some militias.[139]

In 1989 The United Nations passed the Convention on the Rights of the Child. Article 38 states that "State parties shall take all feasible measures to ensure that persons who have not attained the age of 15 years do not take a direct part in hostilities." The optional protocol on the involvement of children in armed conflict came into force in 2002 which stipulates that state actors "shall take all feasible measures to ensure that persons below the age of 18 do not take a direct part in hostilities and that they are not compulsorily recruited into their armed forces."[140] The DRC is a signatory of both of these agreements. The official stance taken by UNICEF is that the use of children in armed conflicts is that it is morally reprehensible and illegal.[141]

State reaction

On 19 March 2006, Major Jean-Pierre Biyoyo was sentenced to five years in prison for recruiting and training child soldiers, it was the first time that a court in the DRC had tried, and convicted a soldier for child recruitment.[142]

Figure 18: *A group of demobilized child soldiers in the DRC*

International reaction

According to David M. Rosen, criticism has been levelled at the US over its support to nations which do recruit children into their armed forces. To comply with the Child Soldiers Protection Act (CSPA) in 2009 the State Department listed six nations which were subject to being sanctioned by the act. Burma, Chad, the DRC, Somalia, Sudan and Yemen. On 25 October 2009, Barack Obama waived the restrictions on four of the six nations. As justification for this Obama stated that the nations involved were important in that they co-operated with interests essential to US foreign policy. The reason given for the DRC exemption was "a need to continue defense reform services and to influence the negative behaviour patterns of the military into a non-political professional force respectful of human rights." Obama also said that all four of these nations were making advances in the elimination of the use of children. However in the DRC child recruitment may actually be on the increase.[143]

A report by MONUSCO confirmed that all parties to the conflict were recruiting girls as child soldiers, and that these children were frequently raped, or used as sex slaves or bush wives by groups such as the Union of Congolese Patriots (UPC) and Patriotic Forces for the Liberation of Congo (FPLC).[144]

Proceedings of the ICC

Thomas Lubanga Dyilo, who was leader of the UPC, a group which operated in the Ituri region in the Northeast of the DRC, was indicted by the ICC in 2006 on three counts of war crimes, recruitment, conscription, and the use of children under 15 in combat.[145] According to Michael Bochenek, who is the director of Amnesty International's International Law and Policy Program, the "verdict will give pause to those around the world who commit the horrific crime of using and abusing children both on and off the battlefield"[146] Luis Moreno Ocampo has said that the Lubanga was "only the start of cases linked to the years of militia violence in Ituri which has killed thousands and produced more than 600,000 refugees."[147]

Germain Katanga former leader of the Front for Patriotic Resistance of Ituri (FRPI), and Mathieu Ngudjolo Chui were indicted on seven counts of war crimes, and three counts of crimes against humanity in 2008, which included the use of children under 15 years of age being used in combat, by the pre trial chamber of the ICC.[148] Katanga was convicted of having taken part in the Bogoro massacre on 24 February 2003. He was cleared of sexual offenses and the use of child soldiers.[149]

Bibliography

<templatestyles src="Template:Refbegin/styles.css" />

- Bochenek, Michael (14 March 2012). "Landmark ICC verdict over use of child soldiers"[150]. *Amnesty International*. Retrieved 7 April 2014.<templatestyles src="Module:Citation/CS1/styles.css"></templatestyles>
- Bouchet-Saulnier, Françoise (2013). *The Practical Guide to Humanitarian Law* (Third English Language ed.). Rowman & Littlefield. ISBN 978-1442221123.<templatestyles src="Module:Citation/CS1/styles.css"></templatestyles>
- Chikuhwa, Tonderai W. (2009). "The Evolution of the United Nations' Protection Agenda for Children". In Scott Gates; Simon Reich. *Child Soldiers in the Age of Fractured States*. University of Pittsburgh Press. pp. 37–54. ISBN 978-0822960294.<templatestyles src="Module:Citation/CS1/styles.css"></templatestyles>
- Drumbl, Mark A. (2012). *Reimagining Child Soldiers in International Law and Policy*. Oxford University Press. ISBN 978-0199592654.<templatestyles src="Module:Citation/CS1/styles.css"></templatestyles>

- Esack, Farid (2012). "Islam, children, and modernity A Qur'anic perspective". In Marcia J. Bunge. *Children, Adults, and Shared Responsibilities: Jewish, Christian and Muslim Perspectives*. Cambridge University Press. pp. 99–118. ISBN 978-1107011144.<templatestyles src="Module:Citation/CS1/styles.css"></templatestyles>
- Feinstein, Lee; Lindberg, Tod (2009). *Means to an End: U.S. Interest in the International Criminal Court*. Brookings Institution Press. ISBN 978-0815703259.<templatestyles src="Module:Citation/CS1/styles.css"></templatestyles>
- Grover, Sonja C. (2012). *Humanity S Children: ICC Jurisprudence and the Failure to Address the Genocidal Forcible Transfer of Children* (2013 ed.). Springer. ISBN 978-3642325007.<templatestyles src="Module:Citation/CS1/styles.css"></templatestyles>
- "DR Congo warlord Germain Katanga found guilty at ICC"[151]. *BBC*. 7 March 2014. Retrieved 8 April 2014.<templatestyles src="Module:Citation/CS1/styles.css"></templatestyles>
- "Child recruitment remains 'endemic' in DR Congo, UN says in new report"[152]. *United Nations*. 24 October 2013. Retrieved 5 April 2014.<templatestyles src="Module:Citation/CS1/styles.css"></templatestyles>
- Novogrodsky, Noah Benjaman (2013). "After the Horror: Child Soldiers and the Special Court for Sierra Leone". In Charles Chernor Jalloh. *The Sierra Leone Special Court and its Legacy: The Impact for Africa and International Criminal Law*. Cambridge University Press. pp. 361–372. ISBN 978-1107029149.<templatestyles src="Module:Citation/CS1/styles.css"></templatestyles>
- Rakisits, Claude (2008). "Child Soldiers in the East of the Democratic Republic of the Congo"[153]. *Refugee Survey Quarterly*. **27** (4): 108–122. doi: 10.1093/rsq/hdn054[154]. Retrieved 5 April 2014.<templatestyles src="Module:Citation/CS1/styles.css"></templatestyles>
- Rosen, David M. (2012). *Child Soldiers: A Reference Handbook*. ABC-CLIO. ISBN 978-1598845266.<templatestyles src="Module:Citation/CS1/styles.css"></templatestyles>
- Singer, Peter Warren (2006). *Children at War*. University of California Press. ISBN 978-0520248762.<templatestyles src="Module:Citation/CS1/styles.css"></templatestyles>
- Soderlund, Walter C.; Briggs, E. Donald; Najem, Tom Pierre; Roberts, Blake C. (2012). *Africa's Deadliest Conflict: Media Coverage of the Humanitarian Disaster in the Congo & the United Nations Response, 1997-2008*. Wilfrid Laurier University Press. ISBN 978-1554588350.<templatestyles src="Module:Citation/CS1/styles.css"></templatestyles>

- Wessells, Michael G. (2007). *Child Soldiers: From Violence to Protection*. Harvard University Press. ISBN 978-0674023598.<templatestyles src="Module:Citation/CS1/styles.css"></templatestyles>
- Whiteman, Shelly L. (2012). "Child Combatants and Peace Processes Challenges of Inclusion and Exclusion". In Rosemary Sheehan; Helen Rhoades; Nicky Stanley. *Vulnerable Children and the Law: International Evidence for Improving Child Welfare, Child Protection and Children's Rights*. Jessica Kingsley Publishers. pp. 75–124. ISBN 978-1849058681.<templatestyles src="Module:Citation/CS1/styles.css"></templatestyles>

Child suicide bombers in the Israeli–Palestinian conflict

<indicator name="pp-default"> 🔒 </indicator> **Child suicide bombers in the Israeli–Palestinian conflict** refers to the exploitation of children to carry out suicide bombings by Palestinian militant groups. Minors have been recruited to attack Israeli targets, both military and civilian, especially during the Second Intifada from 2000 to 2005. This deliberate involvement of children in armed conflict has been condemned by International human rights organizations.

According to Amnesty International, "Palestinian armed groups have repeatedly shown total disregard for the most fundamental human rights, notably the right to life, by deliberately targeting Israeli civilians and by using Palestinian children in armed attacks. Children are susceptible to recruitment by manipulation or may be driven to join armed groups for a variety of reasons, including a desire to avenge relatives or friends killed by the Israeli army."[155]

History

According to the Coalition to Stop the Use of Child Soldiers "2004 Global Report on the Use of Child Soldiers", there were at least nine documented suicide attacks involving Palestinian minors between October 2000 and March 2004 p. 292. In 2004, the Coalition to Stop the Use of Child Soldiers reported that "there was no evidence of systematic recruitment of children by Palestinian armed groups," also noting that this remains a small fraction of the problem in other conflict zones such as Africa, where there are an estimated 20,000 children involved in active combat roles in the Sudan alone.Wikipedia:Citing sources Human Rights Watch also reported that "there was no evidence that the Palestinian Authority (PA) recruited or used child soldiers."

According to the Palestinian Human Rights Monitoring Group, in the al-Aqsa Intifada, children were used as "messengers and couriers, and in some cases as fighters and suicide bombers in attacks on Israeli soldiers and civilians" during the al-Aqsa Intifada. Fatah, Hamas, Palestinian Islamic Jihad Movement and the Popular Front for the Liberation of Palestine have all been implicated in involving children in this way. The issue was brought to world attention after a widely televised incident in which a mentally handicapped Palestinian teenager, Hussam Abdo, was disarmed at an Israeli checkpoint. The youngest Palestinian suicide bomber who blew himself up was Issa Bdeir, a 16-year-old high school student from the village of Al Doha. He blew himself up in a park in Rishon LeZion, killing a teenage boy and an elderly man.

According to the Israel Defense Forces, 29 suicide attacks were carried out by youth under the age of 18 in 2000–2003. From May 2001, 22 shootings attacks and attacks using explosive devices were carried out by youth under the age of 18, and more than 40 youths under the age of 18 were involved in attempted suicide bombings that were thwarted (three in 2004).

On March 29, 2002, Ayat al-Akhras, an 18-year-old girl from the Deheishe Refugee Camp near Bethlehem, detonated explosives strapped around her waist in a supermarket in Jerusalem, killing herself, a 17-year-old Israeli girl named Rachel Levy, and a 55-year-old security guard named Haim Smadar.

On March 24, 2004, one week after capturing a bomb in the bag of 12-year-old Abdullah Quran, Hussam Abdo, a 16-year-old Palestinian (who initially claimed he was 14), was captured in a checkpoint near Nablus wearing an explosive belt. The young boy was paid by the Tanzim militia to detonate himself at the checkpoint. IDF soldiers manning the checkpoint were suspicious of him and told him to stay away from people. Later, an EOD team arrived and by using a police-sapper robot, removed the explosive belt from him. Hussam explained that he was offered 100 NIS and sex with virgins if he would perform the task. He said his friends mocked him in class.

On May 30, 2004, *The New York Times* reported Israeli allegations that the al-Aqsa Martyrs' Brigades were using children to recruit classmates as suicide bombers, and that one child, Nasser Awartani, 15, of Nablus allegedly recruited four of his classmates, one of whom was claimed by the Shabak report on Awartani to be Hussam Abdo.Greg Myre (May 30, 2004). "Israel Says Children Are Used to Recruit Bombers"[156]. *The New York Times*. Retrieved September 5, 2014.<templatestyles src="Module:Citation/CS1/styles.css"></templatestyles>

On June 16, 2004, two girls, aged 14 and 15, were arrested by the IDF for allegedly plotting a suicide bombing. According to an IDF statement, the two children were recruited by activists from Tanzim (Fatah's armed wing), guided by Hezbollah.

On July 3, the Israeli Security Forces thwarted a suicide bombing that it claimed was to have been carried out by 16-year-old Muataz Takhsin Karini. Karini and two of his operators were arrested, while a 12 kg explosive belt was detonated safely by an Israeli EOD crew. On June 5, IDF forces detonated two explosive belts concealed in schoolbags. On July 14, the Shin Bet arrested in Kfar Maskha a suicide bomber. The bomber was identified as 17-year-old Ahmed Bushkar from Nablus.

On September 23, 2004, a day before Yom Kippur, the Shin Bet and the Israel Police announced their capture of a 15-year-old suicide bomber and a 7 kg explosive belt in the village of Dir-Hana in the Western Galilee. The 15-year-old was part of joint terrorist cell of Tanzim and Palestinian Islamic Jihad from Yamon village near Jenin. The four were Palestinians who worked illegally in Israel. The 15-year-old was allegedly paid 1000 shekels in order to blow himself up in Afula.

According to a Shabak report published on September 26, 2004, about 292 Palestinian children have been involved in terrorism.

On September 27, 2004, a 15-year-old suspected suicide bomber was arrested in Nablus. On October 28, Ayub Maaruf, a 16-year-old Fatah suicide bomber, was arrested near Nablus along with his operator.

On November 1, 16-year-old Aamer Alfar blew himself up in Tel Aviv's Carmel Market, killing 3 Israelis in a suicide bombing that was claimed by the Popular Front for the Liberation of Palestine. Alfar's mother and father condemned what they saw as the exploitation of their son:

> God will curse those who recruited Amar. I had heard the stories about recruiting children in Nablus but I didn't think they were true... Yes, it is difficult here for everyone because of the occupation, and life in Nablus is intolerable, but children should not be exploited in this way.Wikipedia:Citation needed

On November 4, a 15-year-old suicide bomber was arrested in Nablus.

On February 3, 2005, Mahmoud Tabouq, a 15- or 16-year-old Palestinian, was arrested at the Huwara checkpoint near Nablus carrying a bag containing an explosive belt, an improvised gun, and 20 bullets. The belt was detonated safely by a Magav bomb squad.[157]

On April 12, a 15-year-old Palestinian boy identified as Hassan Hashash was caught at Huwara checkpoint hiding five pipe bombs under his coat. He tried to ignite them with a match when the soldiers apprehended him. Later he was disarmed, and sappers detonated the bombs safely. Family members of

Hashash suggested that he deliberately carried bombs into an IDF checkpoint in order to be arrested and study for the "Bagrut" final exams in the Israeli jail. A week later, another Palestinian youth (aged 17) was caught carrying explosives in Beit Furik checkpoint.

On April 27, two teenagers, aged 15 (though other sources cite their ages as 12 and 13), were arrested at a checkpoint near Jenin after 11 explosive charges were found on them. One teenager was recruited by the Palestinian Islamic Jihad and the other by the al-Aqsa Martyrs' Brigades. The two told interrogators that they had been acting as couriers for terrorists, but security forces suspect they planned to get close to the soldiers and then detonate the charges.

On May 22, Iad Ladi, a 14- or 15-year-old Palestinian suicide bomber was arrested at a Huwara checkpoint near Nablus. This was the 14th time during April and May that a Palestinian child was arrested as a bomber or a courier. Two days later, another 15-year-old Palestinian teen carrying two pipe bombs, was caught at the same checkpoint. On June 15, The Israeli press reported that the Shabak arrested a Palestinian militant cell in Nablus during the previous month. The cell included eight members, four of whom were child suicide bombers. The cell was on the verge of committing another suicide bombing attack using the four children. According to the Shin Bet, the cell was directed and funded by the Fatah's Tanzim branch and the Lebanese group Hezbollah.

On October 11, a 14-year-old Palestinian boy was arrested by IDF forces. He told the soldiers he was forced to agree to commit a suicide bombing when two terrorists from Fatah's Tanzim faction threatened to murder him by spreading a leaflet accusing him of collaboration unless he agreed. They took pictures of him with a gun and the Qur'an and forced him to write his own will.

On August 27, a 15-year-old Palestinian boy carrying two explosive devices on his body was arrested in the northern Gaza Strip after he attempted to carry out an attack against soldiers operating in the area against Palestinians launching Qassam rockets on Israeli civilians across the border inside Israel.

Use of indoctrination

According to emeritus professor of psychiatry at the University of Virginia School of Medicine Vamik Volkan,

> *Most suicide bombers in the Middle East are chosen as teenagers, "educated", and then sent off to perform their duty when they are in their late teens or early to mid-twenties. The "education" is most effective when religious elements of the large-group identity are provided as solutions for the personal sense of helplessness, shame, and humiliation. Replacing*

borrowed elements sanctioned by God for one's internal world makes that person omnipotent and supports the individual's narcissism.

I found that there was little difficulty in finding young men interested in becoming suicide bombers in Gaza and the West Bank. Repeated actual and expected events humiliate youngsters and interfere with their adaptive identifications with their parents because their parents are humiliated as well.[158]

Volkan gives the examples of beatings, torture, or the loss of a parent as typical humiliating events that might make a young person more susceptible to recruitment for suicide terrorism.

Once recruited, children and teenagers are encouraged to cut off contact with "real world" affairs and subjected to an intense program of memorization and repetition of the Qur'an based more on sound than on meaning.

The typical technique of creating Middle Eastern Muslim suicide bombers includes two basic steps: first, the "teachers" find young people whose personal identity is already disturbed and who are seeking an outer "element" to internalize so they can stabilize their internal world. Second, they develop a "teaching method" that "forces" the large-group identity, ethnic and/or religious, into the "cracks" of the person's damaged or subjugated individual identity. Once people become candidates to be suicide bombers, the routine rules and regulations, so to speak, or individual psychology does not fully apply to their patterns of thought and action.

Anne Speckhard, adjunct associate Professor of Psychiatry, Georgetown University Medical Center and Professor of Psychology, Vesalius College, Free University of Brussels, writes:

In the Palestinian territories, there currently exists a "cult of martyrdom". From a very young age children are socialized into a group consciousness that honors "martyrs", including human bombers who have given their lives for the fight against what is perceived by Palestinians to be the unjust occupation of their lands. Young children are told stories of "martyrs". Many young people wear necklaces venerating particular "martyrs", posters decorate the walls of towns and rock and music videos extol the virtues of bombers. Each act of suicide terrorism is also marked by a last testament and video, which are prepared ahead of time by the "martyr" who can later reach great popularity when the video is played on television. Despite the very deep and real grief of the family and friends left behind, the funerals of "martyrs" are generally accompanied with much fanfare by community and sponsoring organization. Often, the effect of this is confusing to outsiders as it can disrupt, delay and even circumvent the family's ability to focus on its grief over the loss of a family member and it may even support the family in claiming to outsiders joy over the loss of its loved one. This "cult of martyrdom", which has a strong underpinning in longstanding cultural roots (the honoring of martyrs), appears to have developed principally over the last decade, as the first act of suicide terrorism occurred in Israel only twelve years ago.

Umm Nidal, who sent three of her sons, including one 17-year-old, on suicide attacks, said "I love my children, but as Muslims we pressure ourselves and sacrifice our emotions for the interest of the homeland. The greater interest takes precedence to the personal interest." She was later elected to the Palestinian legislature on the Hamas ticket. According to Human Rights Watch,

Major Palestinian armed groups, including Al-Aqsa Martyrs Brigade, the Popular Front for the Liberation of Palestine, Islamic Jihad, and Hamas, have publicly disavowed the use of children in military operations, but those stated policies have not always been implemented. Some leaders, including representatives of Islamic Jihad and Hamas, have said that they consider children of 16 to be adults. International law defines a child as any person under the age of eighteen. [...] Israeli government policy in the Occupied Territories defines Palestinians under the age of 16 as minors while Israeli children in the same territories are considered minors until they reach the age of 18.

According to Islamic tradition, Muslim males are regarded as adults at the age of fifteen.

Baby Suicide Bomber photo

The Baby Suicide Bomber refers to a photo that received media attention in 2002.

During a search done June 29, 2002, of a house belonging to a Hamas militant in the town of Hebron, The IDF claims to have found a photo showing an 18-month infant standing wide-eyed in a baby suit, Red wires strapped to his waist, with a pretend explosives belt, and across his head tied a red bandana of Hamas.

According to BBC News the baby's grandfather, Redwan Abu Turki, said that the dressing of the infant baby as a bomber was from a rally at the university and "the picture was taken just for the fun of it."

Israeli newspapers published the photograph under headlines such as "Terror in Diapers"[159] and "Born to Kill".[160] Israeli Prime Minister Sharon's advisor Dore Gold said the picture "symbolizes the hatred and incitement which the Palestinian leadership has been feeding a whole generation of Palestinian youths." At the U.S. State Department, spokesman Richard Boucher stated that he considered the image as "a highly objectionable display".[161]

While Palestinian officials dismissed it as a propaganda trick, *Haaretz* reported that a Palestinian journalist in the Hebron area said she did not believe the picture was a fake and expressed surprise at the furor it caused in Israel

<templatestyles src="Template:Quote/styles.css"/>

> *"I can find you many, many photos like this," she said. "Many kids imitate adults and wear toy masks and guns, especially during marches. It's not strange at all". She added that she had seen children as young as the one in the photograph wearing similar costumes: "In our society it happens a lot. It's a kind of phenomenon."*

Other photos of children dressed up as militants have been published since then.

Further reading

- Landau, Elaine (2007). *Suicide Bombers: Foot Soldiers of the Terrorist Movement*. Twenty-First Century Books. <templatestyles src="Module:Citation/CS1/styles.css" />ISBN 0-7613-3470-X
- Greenberger, Robert (2007). *Suicide Bombers (In the News)*. Rosen Publishing Group. ISBN 978-1404209770.<templatestyles src="Module:Citation/CS1/styles.css"></templatestyles>
- Bloom, Mia (2005). *Dying to Kill: The Allure of Suicide Terror*. New York: Columbia University Press. ISBN 978-0231133210.<templatestyles src="Module:Citation/CS1/styles.css"></templatestyles>
- Carpenter, Charli R. (2006). *Innocent Women And Children: Gender, Norms and the Protection of Civilians*. Ashgate Publishing, Ltd. <templatestyles src="Module:Citation/CS1/styles.css" />ISBN 0-7546-4745-5
- Charny, Israel W. (2006). *Fighting Suicide Bombing: A Worldwide Campaign for Life*. Greenwood Press. <templatestyles src="Module:Citation/CS1/styles.css" />ISBN 0-275-99336-1

External links

- The Children's Rights Institute[162]
- Suicide Bombers[163] by Vamik D. Volkan of the University of Virginia
- Jeremy Cooke (July 18, 2001). "School trains suicide bombers"[164]. BBC News.<templatestyles src="Module:Citation/CS1/styles.css"></templatestyles>

- Cameron W. Barr (April 1, 2002). "Why a Palestinian girl now wants to be a suicide bomber"[165]. *The Christian Science Monitor*.<templatestyles src="Module:Citation/CS1/styles.css"></templatestyles>
- Justus Weiner. "The Recruitment of Children in Current Palestinian Strategy"[166]. Jerusalem Center for Public Affairs.<templatestyles src="Module:Citation/CS1/styles.css"></templatestyles>
- Ayesha Nasir, author. *Becoming a Child Suicide Bomber*[167]. Video Journalism Movement. Archived from the original[168] on February 8, 2013.<templatestyles src="Module:Citation/CS1/styles.css"></templatestyles> In southern Punjab, madrassas facilitate the recruitment of children into militant groups to learn to become suicide bombers.

Child soldiers in India

Part of a series on
Child soldiers
Main articles
• Child soldiers • History of child soldiers • Impact • Rehabilitation and reintegration
Issues
• Child abduction • Child sexual abuse • Forced marriage • Forced prostitution • Post traumatic stress disorder
Instances (examples)
• World War II • Africa • Central African Republic • Democratic Republic of Congo • India • Myanmar • Sierra Leone • Somalia • Sri Lanka
Legal aspects
• Paris Principles • Convention on the Rights of the Child • Optional protocol
Movement to end the use of child soldiers

- Red Hand Day
- $\underline{v}$
- $\underline{t}$
- $\underline{e}$[169]

According to Peter Singer the use of **child soldiers in India** is a common occurrence and that up to seventeen militant factions use child soldiers in the Kashmir region. Radha Kumar says that nations which have massive poverty and are heavily reliant on an agricultural economy will produce militants which are usually uneducated and that in a region where a conflict is protracted, the use of child soldiers becomes a common occurrence. According to a report from the Conflict Study Center, child soldiers are used in Assam, Manipur, Nagaland, Andhra Pradesh, Chhattisgarh, Jharkhand, Karnataka, Maharashtra and Jammu and Kashmir; and that children were used by both the state and insurgents. Child soldiers also serve in the Indian armed forces. The use of child soldiers by the state and by non state actors is a violation of the Geneva convention and the Convention on the Rights of the Child

Chhattisgarh

In Chhattisgarh state, it is estimated that up to 90,000 children are involved in the ongoing Naxalite insurgency. The majority of children are used by militants, though government supported militias also use them. The Asian Legal Resource Centre has stated that human rights groups have voiced concerns over the use of child soldiers by the state and the Naxalites. According to them, up to 118 districts in India are facing armed insurrection and that child soldiers were used by both sides in these conflicts. Human rights watch has also accused the Indian security forces of using children as spies and messengers, although the Indian government denies this allegation. The Coalition to Stop the Use of Child Soldiers report in 2008 stated that there was recruitment of children by state backed groups in the region. although the majority of child soldiers were used by militants.

Appendix

References

[1] //en.wikipedia.org/w/index.php?title=Template:Child_soldiers&action=edit

[2] //en.wikipedia.org/w/index.php?title=Template:War&action=edit

[3] //en.wikipedia.org/w/index.php?title=Template:Slavery&action=edit

[4] Norman Davies, *Rising '44: The Battle for Warsaw*, https://books.google.com/books?id=Jzxt9FFBDPwC&pg=PA603 Pan Books 2004 p.603

[5] Michael Leggiere, The Fall of Napoleon: The Allied Invasion of France 1813–1814, pg.99–100

[6] Stephen Pope, Dictionary of the Napoleonic Wars, p. 318

[7] Slinger, P. W. Children at War. New York: Pantheon Books, 2005.

[8] Momčilo Gavrić – najmlađi vojnik Prvog svetskog rata http://www.novosti.rs/vesti/naslovna/drustvo/aktuelno.290.html:451827-Momcilo-Gavric---najmladji-vojnik-Prvog-svetskog-rata ("Večernje novosti", 31 August 2013)

[9] Child soldiers global report 2004: Africa Regional overview https://web.archive.org/web/20091226221427/http://www.child-soldiers.org/document/get?id=743, Child Soldiers International http://www.child-soldiers.org/contact/contact .

[10] //en.wikipedia.org/w/index.php?title=History_of_children_in_the_military&action=edit

[11] Child soldiers global report 2004: Africa Regional overview https://web.archive.org/web/20091226221427/http://www.child-soldiers.org/document/get?id=743, Child Soldiers International http://www.child-soldiers.org/contact/contact .

[12] Child soldiers global report 2004: Africa Regional overview https://web.archive.org/web/20091226221427/http://www.child-soldiers.org/document/get?id=743, Child Soldiers International http://www.child-soldiers.org/contact/contact .

[13] , press release from the Special Court for Sierra Leone, 20 June 2007; "Sierra Leone Convicts 3 of War Crimes" https://www.washingtonpost.com/wp-dyn/content/article/2007/06/20/AR2007062000952.html?hpid=moreheadlines , *Associated Press*, 20 June 2007 (hosted by *The Washington Post*);

[14] Yasmin Anwar Damning report on Uganda war crimes http://berkeley.edu/news/media/releases/2007/06/15_LRA.shtml , UC Berkeley NewsCenter http://www.berkeley.edu/misc/newscenter-feedback.shtml

[15] Hammond Atlas of the 20th Century (1999) P. 134-5

[16] Dunnigan, A Quick and Dirty Guide to War (1991)

[17] Dictionary of Twentieth Century World History, by Jan Palmowski (Oxford, 1997)

[18] Clodfelter, Michael, Warfare and Armed Conflict: A Statistical Reference to Casualty and Other Figures, 1618–1991

[19] Chirot, Daniel: *Modern Tyrants: The Power and Prevalence of Evil in Our Age* (1994)

[20] "B&J": Jacob Bercovitch and Richard Jackson, *International Conflict: A Chronological Encyclopedia of Conflicts and Their Management 1945–1995* (1997) p. 195

[21] Bureau Report *LTTE rebels make child recruitment illegal: Report http://www.zeenews.com/znnew/articles.asp?aid=331811&sid=SAS* , Zee News 27 October 2006

[22] Child Soldiers International p. 217

[23] http://childsoldiersworldindex.org/

[24] https://www.child-soldiers.org/shop/global-report-2001

[25] https://www.child-soldiers.org/Shop/global-report-2004-1

[26] https://www.child-soldiers.org/Shop/global-report-2008-1

[27] https://www.child-soldiers.org/shop/louder-than-words-1

[28] //en.wikipedia.org/w/index.php?title=Template:Child_soldiers&action=edit

[29] National Scientific Council on the Developing Child. (2005/2014). *Excessive Stress Disrupts the Architecture of the Developing Brain: Working Paper 3*. Updated Edition. http://www.developingchild.harvard.edu

[30] Article 49 http://www.unhchr.ch/html/menu3/b/k2crc.htm. (Deadlink)

[31] Article 47 http://www.unhchr.ch/html/menu3/b/k2crc.htm.

[32]//en.wikipedia.org/w/index.php?title=Template:Youth_rights_sidebar&action=edit

[33]

[34]

[35]Amnesty International USA (2007). *Convention on the Rights of the Child: Frequently Asked Questions* http://www.amnestyusa.org/children/crn_faq.html . Retrieved 26 November 2008.

[36]General Comment 8 http://www.unhchr.ch/tbs/doc.nsf/ 898586b1dc7b4043c1256a450044f331/6545c032cb57bff5c12571fc002e834d/$FILE/ G0740771.pdf, Committee on the Rights of the Child.

[37]Article 19, Convention on the Rights of the Child.

[38]Sutherland, Elaine E. (2003). "Can International Conventions Drive Domestic Law Reform? The Case of Physical Punishment of Children" in Dewar J., Parker S. (eds.) *Family law: processes, practices, pressures: proceedings of the Tenth World Conference of the International Society of Family Law*, July 2000, Brisbane, Australia. Oxford: Hart, p. 488.

[39]French reaction to the execution of Delera Darabi, May 2009 https//web.archive.org ; European Union's reaction to the execution of Delera Darabi, May 2009 https//web.archive.org.

[40]Children's Rights Alliance website http://www.childrensrights.ie/convention.php .

[41]O'Brien, Carl (28 September 2006). "UN to seek changes in Constitution in support of children". *Irish Times* (Dublin).

[42]Or Kashti (21 November 2010). "UNICEF: Israel negligent in guarding children's rights http://www.haaretz.com/print-edition/news/unicef-israel-negligent-in-guarding-children-s-rights-1.325790". *Haaretz* (Tel Aviv).

[43]Children suffering devastating and lasting impact of Gaza crisis, says UN Committee on the Rights of the Child http://www.ohchr.org/en/NewsEvents/Pages/DisplayNews.aspx?NewsID= 12818&LangID=E, United Nations Commission on Human Rights, 22 November 2012.

[44]United Nations Treaty Collection https://treaties.un.org/Pages/ViewDetails.aspx?src= TREATY&mtdsg_no=IV-11&chapter=4&lang=en .

[45]*Tavita v Minister of Immigration*, 17 December 1993 [1994] 2 NZLR 257 at 265, cited in Ferdinandusse, Ward N., *Direct Application of International Criminal Law in National Courts*, Cambridge University Press, 2006, p. 161.

[46]*Saudi Arabia: Follow U.N. Call to End Juvenile Death Penalty* http://hrw.org/english/docs/ 2006/01/29/saudia12546.htm, Human Rights Watch, 28 January 2006.

[47]Frost, Nick, *Child Welfare: Major Themes in Health and Social Welfare*, Taylor and Francis, 2004, p. 175; Routledge, 2005,

[48]Davies, Martin, *The Blackwell Encyclopaedia of Social Work*, Blackwell, 2000, p. 354.

[49]Easton, Mark (19 September 2008). "UK to give up child rights opt-outs" http://www.bbc. co.uk/blogs/thereporters/markeaston/2008/09/uk_to_give_up_child_rights_opt.html. *BBC reporters blog*.

[50]Harvey, Colin J., *Human Rights in the Community: Rights As Agents For Change*, Oxford: Hart, 2005, p. 234.

[51]Hughes, Beverley, Minister for Children, Young People and Families, "Article defending the Government's position on smacking" http://www.dcsf.gov.uk/pns/DisplayPN.cgi?pn_id= 2008_0224, press release, 8 October 2008.

[52]Evidence to the Joint Committee on Human Rights https://publications.parliament.uk/pa/ jt200203/jtselect/jtrights/96/96a04.htm, UK Parliament, 12 May 2003.

[53]House of Lords and House of Commons Joint Committee on Human Rights, The UN Convention on the Rights of the Child https://publications.parliament.uk/pa/jt200203/jtselect/jtrights/ 117/117.pdf, Tenth Report of Session 2002–03, page 55.

[54]"Government Responses to Reports from the Committee" https://publications.parliament.uk/ pa/jt200506/jtselect/jtrights/104/104.pdf, Session 2005-06, paras. 82, 85, 86: HL 104, HC 850.

[55]Smolin, David M. "Overcoming Religious Objections to the Convention on the Rights of the Child" http://www.law.emory.edu/cms/site/fileadmin/journals/eilr/v20n1/SmolinCROP.pdf, *Emory International Law Review*, vol.20, p. 83.

[56]"Human Rights and Social Issues at the U.N.: A Guide for U.S. Policymakers" http://www. heritage.org/Research/WorldwideFreedom/bg1965.cfm, *Heritage Foundation*

[57]US Supreme Court: *Roper v. Simmons*, No. 03-633: 1 March 2005

[58]Miller v. Alabama certiori to the Court of Criminal Appeals of Alabama, No. 10-9646 (Argued 20 March 2012 - Decided 25 June 2012)

[59]Walden University Presidential Youth Debate http://debate.waldenu.edu/video/question-12/ #content , October 2008.

[60]Podgers, "The Last Holdout," ABA Journal at 84 (March 2016)

[61]

[62]

[63]http://www.ohchr.org/EN/ProfessionalInterest/Pages/CRC.aspx

[64]https://web.archive.org/web/20140211151110/https://treaties.un.org/pages/viewdetails.aspx? src=treaty&mtdsg_no=iv-11&chapter=4&lang=en

[65]http://www.unicef.org/crc/

[66]http://legal.un.org/avl/ha/crc/crc.html

[67]http://legal.un.org/avl/historicarchives.html

[68]https://web.archive.org/web/20090729071013/http://www.crin.org/docs/resources/treaties/crc. 25/annex-vi-crin.asp

[69]http://www.leader-values.com/Content/detail.asp?ContentDetailID=794

[70]http://childrensrightsportal.org/convention/

[71]http://www.everychild.ca/

[72]//en.wikipedia.org/w/index.php?title=Template:Child_soldiers&action=edit

[73]http://www.unicef.org/media/media_38208.html, UNICEF press release

[74]http://www.unicef.org/protection/files/Attendees.pdf, List of attendees

[75]http://www.diplomatie.gouv.fr/en/france-priorities_1/democracy-human-rights_1101/ children-rights_3265/paris-commitments_8658.html

[76]http://www.unicef.org/media/files/ParisPrinciples_EN.pdf

[77]http://child-soldiers.org

[78]//en.wikipedia.org/w/index.php?title=Template:Child_soldiers&action=edit

[79]Norman Davies, *Rising '44: The Battle for Warsaw,* https://books.google.com/books?id= Jzxt9FFBDPwC&pg=PA603 Pan Books 2004 p.603

[80]ICRC Commentary on Protocol I: Article 77 http://www.icrc.org/ihl.nsf/COM/470-750099? OpenDocument website of the ICRC ¶ 3183–3191 also ¶ 3171 http://www.icrc.org/ihl.nsf/ COM/470-750098?OpenDocument

[81]http://www.ohchr.org/EN/ProfessionalInterest/Pages/OPACCRC.aspx

[82]http://treaties.un.org/Pages/ViewDetails.aspx?src=TREATY&mtdsg_no=IV-11-b&chapter= 4&lang=en

[83]http://www.unicef.org/publications/files/option_protocol_conflict.pdf

[84]//en.wikipedia.org/w/index.php?title=Template:Child_soldiers&action=edit

[85]//en.wikipedia.org/w/index.php?title=Template:War&action=edit

[86]//en.wikipedia.org/w/index.php?title=Template:Slavery&action=edit

[87]

[88]Norman Davies, *Rising '44: The Battle for Warsaw,* https://books.google.com/books?id= Jzxt9FFBDPwC&pg=PA603 Pan Books 2004 p.603

[89]

[90]

[91]

[92]Betancourt, Theresa S.; Borisova, Ivelina I.; de la Soudière, Marie; Williamson, John (2011). "Sierra Leone's Child Soldiers: War Exposures and Mental Health Problems by Gender". *Journal of Adolescent Health.* **49** (1): 21–28 – via Elsevier Science Direct.

[93]Verhey, Beth (2004). *Reaching the Girls: Study on Girls Associated with Armed Forces and Groups.* Save the Children UK and the NGO Group: CARE, IFESH and IRC. Retrieved 21 February 2017.

[94]Save the Children. *Forgotten Casualties of War: Girls in armed conflict.* 2005. Retrieved 21 February 2017.

[95]Mazurana, Dyan E.; McKay, Susan A.; Carlson, Khristopher C.; Kasper, Janel C. (2002). "Girls in Fighting Forces and Groups: Their Recruitment, Participation, Demobilization, and Reintegration". *Peace and Conflict: Journal of Peace Psychology.* **8** (2): 97–123 – via OhioLINK.

[96] //en.wikipedia.org/w/index.php?title=Rehabilitation_and_reintegration_of_child_soldiers&action=edit

[97] https://www.child-soldiers.org/reintegration

[98] //en.wikipedia.org/w/index.php?title=Template:Child_soldiers&action=edit

[99] Rakisits 2008 pp 108-122

[100] Child soldiers global report 2004: Africa Regional overview https://web.archive.org/web/20091226221427/http://www.child-soldiers.org/document/get?id=743, Child Soldiers International http://www.child-soldiers.org/contact/contact.

[101] Beah, Ishmael. *A Long Way Gone: Memoirs of a Boy Soldier.* Penguin, 2013.

[102] United Nations 2014.

[103] Singer 2006, p. 21.

[104] Whiteman 2012, p. 80.

[105] MONUSCO 2013.

[106] Drumbl 2012, p. 32.

[107] Horeman, B. & Stolwijk, M., Refusing to Bear Arms: A World Survey of Conscription and Conscientious Objection to Military Service, War Resisters International, London, 1998; The question of conscientious objection to military service: Report of the SecretaryGeneral prepared pursuant to Commission resolution 1995/83, UN Doc. E/CN.4/1997/99, 16 January 1997; IISS.

[108] *Political Parties of the World* (6th edition, 2005), ed. Bogdan Szajkowski

[109] //en.wikipedia.org/w/index.php?title=Child_soldiers_in_Africa&action=edit

[110] https://plato.stanford.edu/archives/sum2015/entries/justice-retributive/#AppRetJus

[111] https://www.sagepub.com/sites/default/files/upm-binaries/5144_Banks_II_Proof_Chapter_5.pdf

[112] http://www.un.org/en/events/peacekeepersday/2003/docs/ddr.htm

[113] http://siteresources.worldbank.org/EXTSOCIALDEVELOPMENT/Resources/244362-1164107274725/DDRFinal3-print.pdf

[114] https//www.oecd.org

[115] http://www.peaceau.org/en/page/68-disarmament-demobilization-and-reintegration-ddr

[116] https://theconversation.com/how-child-soldiers-are-recruited-from-refugee-camps-2938

[117] http://psycnet.apa.org/doiLanding?doi=10.1207%2FS15327949PAC0802_01

[118] Steel, Michelle. "Child Soldiers" http://www.vision.org/visionmedia/social-issues/child-soldiers/6684.aspx Social Issues: Child Soldiers, 2008.

[119] https://www.child-soldiers.org/democratic-republic-of-congo

[120] https://invisiblechildren.com/our-work/

[121] https://www.unicef.org/protection/57929_58007.html

[122] https://www.unicef.org/wcaro/nigeriaregionalcrisis/WCAR.Migration.July2017.LRe.pdf

[123] http://culturesofresistance.org/end-child-soldiers

[124] https://childsoldiersworldindex.org

[125] https://www.un.org/apps/news/story.asp?NewsID=46330#.U0AIUKhdXO8

[126] http://rsq.oxfordjournals.org/content/27/4/108.abstract

[127] //doi.org/10.1093%2Frsq%2Fhdn054

[128] https://www.un.org/apps/news/story.asp?NewsID=46954&Cr=central+african+republic&Cr1

[129] //en.wikipedia.org/w/index.php?title=Template:Child_soldiers&action=edit

[130] http://child-soldiers.org

[131] http://unicef.org

[132] //en.wikipedia.org/w/index.php?title=Template:Child_soldiers&action=edit

[133] Whiteman 2012, p. 80.

[134] Drumbl 2012, p. 32.

[135] MONUSCO 2013.

[136] Singer 2006, p. 21.

[137] Novogrodsky 2013, p. 368.

[138] Rakisits 2008, pp. 108-122.

[139] Wessells 2007, p. 12.

[140] Esack 2012, pp. 115-116.

[141] Rosen 2012, pp. 22-23.

[142] Chikuhwa 2009, p. 48.

[143] Rosen 2012, pp. 89-90.

[144] Grover 2012, p. 117.

[145] Feinstein 2009, pp. 65-66.

[146] Bochenek 2012.

[147] Soderlund et al. 2012, p. 105.

[148] Bouchet-Saulnier 2013, p. 51.

[149] Katanga 2014.

[150] https://www.amnesty.org/en/news/landmark-icc-verdict-over-use-child-soldiers-2012-03-14

[151] https://www.bbc.co.uk/news/world-africa-26477680

[152] https://www.un.org/apps/news/story.asp?NewsID=46330#.U0AIUKhdXO8

[153] http://rsq.oxfordjournals.org/content/27/4/108.abstract

[154] //doi.org/10.1093%2Frsq%2Fhdn054

[155] "Israel/Occupied Territories: Palestinian armed groups must not use children." Amnesty International. Public Statement. Published 23 May 2005. Accessed October 2015. https://web.archive.org/web/20090906152355/http://asiapacific.amnesty.org/library/Index/ENGMDE150332005?open&of=ENG-ISR

[156] https://www.nytimes.com/2004/05/30/international/middleeast/30teen.html?module=Search&mabReward=relbias%3As%2C{%221%22%3A%22RI%3A5%22}

[157] Video available.

[158] Vamik D. Volkan: Suicide Bombers http://www.akademikortadogu.com/belge/ortadogu8%20makale/vamik_d_volkan.pdf University of Virginia

[159] "Terror in Diapers" (photo caption), Maariv, as cited by Photo of baby suicide bomber called 'a joke' http://archives.cnn.com/2002/WORLD/meast/06/28/baby.photo/index.html, CNN, published June 29, 2002

[160] "Born to kill" (photo caption), *The Jerusalem Post*, June 28, 2002

[161] Excerpts: June 28, 2002 Press Briefing https://www.state.gov/p/nea/rls/rm/11561.htm, The Office of Electronic Information, Bureau of Public Affairs on behalf of the U.S. State Department, June 28, 2002

[162] http://www.childrensrightsinstitute.org/

[163] http://www.akademikortadogu.com/belge/ortadogu8%20makale/vamik_d_volkan.pdf

[164] http://news.bbc.co.uk/2/hi/middle_east/1446003.stm

[165] http://www.csmonitor.com/2002/0401/p07s01-wome.html

[166] http://www.jcpa.org/brief/brief2-8.htm

[167] https://archive.is/20130208234550/http://www.vjmovement.com/truth/465

[168] http://www.vjmovement.com/truth/465

[169] //en.wikipedia.org/w/index.php?title=Template:Child_soldiers&action=edit

Article Sources and Contributors

The sources listed for each article provide more detailed licensing information including the copyright status, the copyright owner, and the license conditions.

History of children in the military *Source:* https://en.wikipedia.org/w/index.php?oldid=863438864 *License:* Creative Commons Attribution-Share Alike 3.0 *Contributors:* 564dude, Aisteco, Applodion, Fugitivedave, Gog the Mild, HistoryReader85, Hohum, Koopinator, LittlePuppers, Noogcat0, Paine Ellsworth, QuiteUnusual, Rathfelder, Samee, TigerDover, 1 anonymous edits 3

Impact of war on children *Source:* https://en.wikipedia.org/w/index.php?oldid=856894358 *License:* Creative Commons Attribution-Share Alike 3.0 *Contributors:* Boghog, Bri, CASSIOPEIA, Choi922, Coffeedrinker115, Divya Bhatnagar, Dodger67, Fugitivedave, Gene Wilson, Gronk Oz, Jbhunley, JzG, Mattg82, Rathfelder, Shalor (Wiki Ed) 25

Convention on the Rights of the Child *Source:* https://en.wikipedia.org/w/index.php?oldid=863619720 *License:* Creative Commons Attribution-Share Alike 3.0 *Contributors:* 1990'sguy, Abhishekdas552, Adisonalex, Alarics, Anarchyte, BD2412, Bgwhite, Bhawani Gautam, Binksternet, Broccoli and Coffee, Canadianknowledgelover, Carolmooredc, Carrot70, Chris Howard, ChrisGualtieri, ClueBot NG, Cnzx, Coreydragon, CsDix, Czar, DFT B3LYP, Da Bes, Danlaycock, DesireeLaPointeUG, Discospinster, Donner60, Doof10, Douglas the Comeback Kid, Enthusiast01, Eraserhead1, Fl6Pres.Potato, Fayenatic london, Flooded with them hundreds, Flyer22 Reborn, FoCuSandLeArN, Fuseau, Future Perfect at Sunrise, Gadyke, Good Olfactory, GraemeL, Grubemeister, GulchinHuseynova, Hairy Dude, Haphill, Hipersons, Hmains, Hollyfield25, Humanrightslawyer1031, I dream of horses, IVONNE SENCEBE, Iainsona, IdiotSavant, J 1982, Jarbie, John Paul Parks, Jonesey95, Joshua, KylieTastic, L.tak, LambdaChi, LdC, Leutha, Licalor, LilyKitty, Lotje, MadelineFF, Magioladitis, Mangokeylime, Marcocapelle, Marek69, Materialscientist, Middayexpress, Mindmatrix, MopTop, Mrsammyqn, Munchkin2013, NFLisAwesome, NPrice, Nonformality, Ponyo, Praxidicae, Puddleglum, RA0808, Raggz, Reaper Eternal, Riceissa, Richard75, Sa.vakilian, Shiremohamed, Simplexity22, Smyth, Sudar123, Sugarcube73, Susandn, Tammiey, That-Vela-Fella, TheJJunk, Throughme, Titodutta, Tl-izama, Tolly4bolly, Totocol, Trcovell, UNAVL, Vanished user 8y2384weihsdjj3kjrd, Vhann, Vigyani, Widr, Yintan, Ylleman, 149 anonymous edits .. 32

Free Children from War conference *Source:* https://en.wikipedia.org/w/index.php?oldid=863788069 *License:* Creative Commons Attribution-Share Alike 3.0 *Contributors:* Bearcat, Fugitivedave, Gog the Mild, Greenhas, Hmains, Malcolma, UsingtheForce 42

Optional Protocol on the Involvement of Children in Armed Conflict *Source:* https://en.wikipedia.org/w/index.php?oldid=861560694 *License:* Creative Commons Attribution-Share Alike 3.0 *Contributors:* Alansohn, Bolivian Unicyclist, Chase Flowers, CommonsDelinker, Cyrus noto3at bulaga, Enquire, Finnusertop, Freechild, Fugitivedave, Goatchurch, Gog the Mild, Good Olfactory, Greenhas, Hipersons, Hmains, Humanrightslawyer1031, Im-paciente, Kai-Hendrik, Kbdank71, L.tak, LilyKitty, Marcocapelle, Neutrality, Nihiltres, Ohconfucius, PBS, PullUpYourSocks, Rich Farmbrough, Samee, Solomonfromfinland, Sustainablefutures2015, That-Vela-Fella, Tim!, Unara, Zingi, 11 anonymous edits 44

Rehabilitation and reintegration of child soldiers *Source:* https://en.wikipedia.org/w/index.php?oldid=863449726 *License:* Creative Commons Attribution-Share Alike 3.0 *Contributors:* Boghog, Fugitivedave, Gog the Mild, Gronk Oz, Hohum, Ira Leviton, Keith D, Maddiemcadams, MensanDel-tiologist, Miax6, Neutrality, Royeniran, Sepulvedalu, Shalor (Wiki Ed), The Mighty Glen, Tom.Reding, Wordsculptor2018, 1 anonymous edits 52

Child soldiers in Africa *Source:* https://en.wikipedia.org/w/index.php?oldid=847996449 *License:* Creative Commons Attribution-Share Alike 3.0 *Contributors:* Alpha3031, Batball69, Brigade Piron, Charles Essie, ClueBot NG, Darkness Shines, Dcirovic, Dimvasilk, Eagle4000, Excirial, Fugitivedave, Gilliam, Haydencombel, Hmains, Jarble, Jdougla6, John of Reading, Jprussak, K6ka, Kekeo1121, Kintetsubuffalo, Malik Shabazz, Mart-inmerati16, Mikeblas, NawlinWiki, Nick Number, OccultZone, Oshwah, RNLockwood, Rathfelder, Runner1928, Saturn star, Sdmoreno, Serols, Shalor (Wiki Ed), Sjö, Spintendo, UsingtheForce, Vanamonde93, Yalmazan, 39 anonymous edits 65

Child soldiers in the Central African Republic *Source:* https://en.wikipedia.org/w/index.php?oldid=839256469 *License:* Creative Commons Attribution-Share Alike 3.0 *Contributors:* Arkon, Darkness Shines, Fugitivedave, Garagepunk66, Gog the Mild, 2 anonymous edits 85

Child soldiers in the Democratic Republic of the Congo *Source:* https://en.wikipedia.org/w/index.php?oldid=846802282 *License:* Creative Commons Attribution-Share Alike 3.0 *Contributors:* Brigade Piron, Charles Essie, Darkness Shines, Darrend1967, Dcirovic, Giraffedata, KKarungu Njue, Oreo Priest, Runner1928, Serols, UsingtheForce, Widr, 10 anonymous edits 89

Child suicide bombers in the Israeli–Palestinian conflict *Source:* https://en.wikipedia.org/w/index.php?oldid=844939240 *License:* Creative Commons Attribution-Share Alike 3.0 *Contributors:* Abu ali, Al Ameer son, Amoruso, Amorymeltzer, AndresHerutJaim, Andrewt, Anomalocaris, AnonMoos, Ashmoo, Avraham, BU Rob13, Baatarsaikan, Bakasuprman, Balagen, Benqish, Bluesquareapple, Boneyard90, Briangotts, Broccoli and Coffee, Can't sleep, clown will eat me, Carcharoth, Carolmooredc, Cesead, ClueBot NG, CommonsDelinker, Dahveed323, Deuterium, Dewritech, Dick Kimball, Dispenser, Egeymi, El C, Eleland, EliteSoul, FayssalF, Flayer, Former user 2, Fratrep, G2bambino, Gaius Cornelius, Gbinal, GcSwRhIc, Gilabrand, Harryboyles, Historicist, Hmains, Hornplease, Humus sapiens, Hypnosadist, Ian Pitchford, IranitGreenberg, Irn, Itzse, J04n, Jaakobou, Jeff G, John of Reading, Jusdafax, Kafziel, Kiore, Koavf, Lihaas, Magioladitis, Marcocapelle, MarkBrowne1888, Marokwitz, MathKnight, Matt57, Montgomery, Moshe Constantine Hassan Al-Silverburg, Mr little irish, Mutandis~enwiki, Nableezy, NatanFlayer, Niceguyedc, Nuwewsco, PaulDocStewart, Pezboy241, Plasticup, Plot Spoiler, Quaiqu, Radagast83, Radical-Dreamer, Reinyday, Reverie98, Rich Farmbrough, Rjwilmsi, Robofish, Sandstein, Sanguinalis, Schmiegestestor, Shrike, Sir Nicholas de Mimsy-Porpington, Sm8900, Soap, Some jerk on the Internet, Srich32977, Tapir Terrific, Tarc, Tassedethe, Tawkerbot2, The Thing That Should Not Be, Thibbs, Threeafterthree, Tiamut, Tommy2010, Umer Al-Amerikee, VJ Movement, Valley2city, WPGA2345, Ynhockey, Yoshm, Zeq, Zzuuzz, Δ, 137 anonymous edits 94

Child soldiers in India *Source:* https://en.wikipedia.org/w/index.php?oldid=842731464 *License:* Creative Commons Attribution-Share Alike 3.0 *Contributors:* Auric, Charles Essie, ClueBot NG, Cpt.a.haddock, Darkness Shines, Ekabhishek, Fugitivedave, Ginsuloft, Jeffrd10, Mar4d, Titodutta, WereSpielChequers, 9 anonymous edits 101

Image Sources, Licenses and Contributors

The sources listed for each image provide more detailed licensing information including the copyright status, the copyright owner, and the license conditions.

License

Index

115

www.ingramcontent.com/pod-product-compliance
Lightning Source LLC
Chambersburg PA
CBHW021148090426
42740CB00008B/1007